CGP scores another winner!

Exams are like sport — you need great preparation and the right mindset
to do well. (Apart from that, exams are not much like sport.)

Luckily, this fantastic CGP book is packed with exam-style questions, covering
everything from basic definitions to those heavyweight 9-mark extended answers.
And there are plenty of data analysis questions too!

We've also included model answers and mark schemes for every question,
plus a full set of mock exams to help you warm up for the real thing!

CGP — still the best! ☺

Our sole aim here at CGP is to produce the highest quality books —
carefully written, immaculately presented and dangerously close to being funny.

Then we work our socks off to get them out to you
— at the cheapest possible prices.

Contents

✓ Use the tick boxes to check off the topics you've completed.

Section One — Anatomy and Physiology

Section Two — Movement Analysis

Section Three — Physical Training

Section Four — Health, Fitness and Well-being

Section Five — Sport Psychology

Section Six — Sport, Society and Culture

Practice Papers

Published by CGP

Editors:
Chris Corrall, Joanna Daniels and Alison Palin.

Contributors:
Steve Ireland

With thanks to Chris Cope and Simon Little for the proofreading.

With thanks to Ana Pungartnik for the copyright research.

Acknowledgements:

With thanks to iStock.com for permission to use the images on pages 5, 6, 57, 60 & 62.

Normative data table for grip dynamometer test on page 25 was published in 'Physical Education and the Study of Sport' 4th ed, 2002, Davis ed, p.123, 1 table ('Normative data table for grip strength test' for 16 to 19 year olds), Copyright Elsevier (2016).

Data about obesity rates on page 40 copyright © 2015, Health and Social Care Information Centre. All rights reserved.

Graphs on pages 40 & 71 contain public sector information licensed under the Open Government Licence v3.0. http://www.nationalarchives.gov.uk/doc/open-government-licence/version/3/

Graphs on pages 49 & 75 based on data from Sport England.

Source for the data about shirt sponsorship in the Premier League on page 50: sportingintelligence.com.

Normative data for vertical jump test on page 56 from ARKINSTALL, M et al. (2010) VCE Physical Education 2. Malaysia: Macmillan. p.248. © Reproduced by permission of Macmillan Education Australia.

How To Use This Book

- Hold the book <u>upright</u>, approximately <u>50 cm</u> from your face, ensuring that the text looks like <u>this</u>, not ज़ाय़त़. Alternatively, place the book on a <u>horizontal</u> surface (e.g. a table or desk) and sit adjacent to the book, at a distance which doesn't make the text too small to read.

- In case of emergency, press the two halves of the book together <u>firmly</u> in order to close.

- Before attempting to use this book, familiarise yourself with the following <u>safety information</u>:

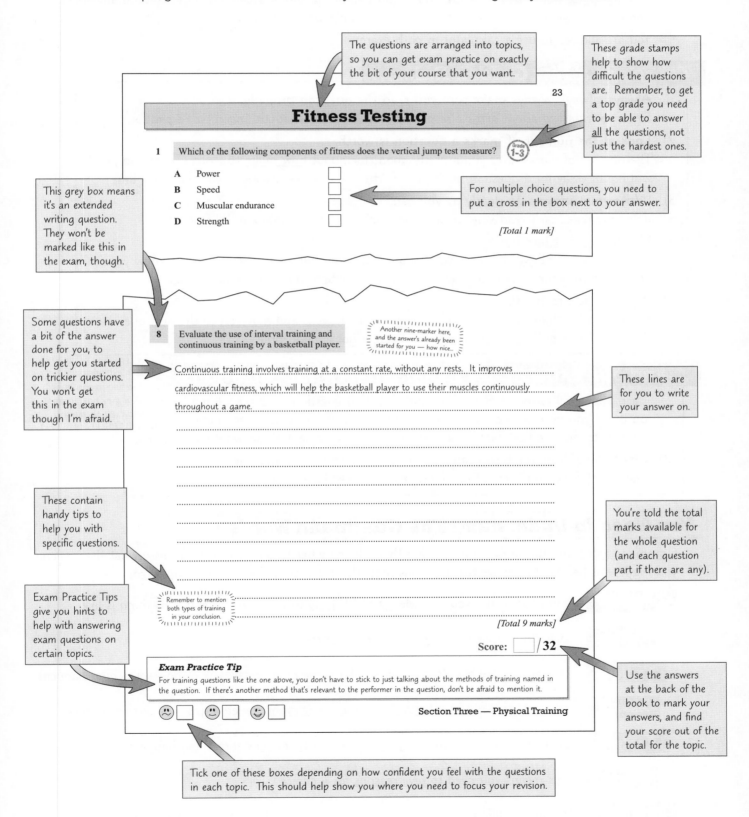

The questions are arranged into topics, so you can get exam practice on exactly the bit of your course that you want.

These grade stamps help to show how difficult the questions are. Remember, to get a top grade you need to be able to answer <u>all</u> the questions, not just the hardest ones.

23

Fitness Testing

1   Which of the following components of fitness does the vertical jump test measure?   Grade 1-3

    A   Power ☐
    B   Speed ☐
    C   Muscular endurance ☐
    D   Strength ☐

[Total 1 mark]

This grey box means it's an extended writing question. They won't be marked like this in the exam, though.

For multiple choice questions, you need to put a cross in the box next to your answer.

8   Evaluate the use of interval training and continuous training by a basketball player.

Another nine-marker here, and the answer's already been started for you — how nice...

Continuous training involves training at a constant rate, without any rests. It improves cardiovascular fitness, which will help the basketball player to use their muscles continuously throughout a game.

Some questions have a bit of the answer done for you, to help get you started on trickier questions. You won't get this in the exam though I'm afraid.

These lines are for you to write your answer on.

These contain handy tips to help you with specific questions.

You're told the total marks available for the whole question (and each question part if there are any).

Exam Practice Tips give you hints to help with answering exam questions on certain topics.

Remember to mention both types of training in your conclusion.

[Total 9 marks]

Score: ☐ /32

Exam Practice Tip
For training questions like the one above, you don't have to stick to just talking about the methods of training named in the question. If there's another method that's relevant to the performer in the question, don't be afraid to mention it.

☹ ☐   ☺ ☐   😀 ☐

Section Three — Physical Training

Use the answers at the back of the book to mark your answers, and find your score out of the total for the topic.

Tick one of these boxes depending on how confident you feel with the questions in each topic. This should help show you where you need to focus your revision.

Exam Tips

Exam Stuff

1) You have to do two exams for your Edexcel GCSE in PE — Components 1 and 2.

2) Component 1 will focus on anatomy and physiology, movement analysis, physical training and data. It will be 1 hour and 45 minutes long and worth 90 marks.

3) Component 2 will focus on health, fitness and well-being, sport psychology, socio-cultural influences and data. It will be 1 hour and 15 minutes long and worth 70 marks.

4) You are allowed to use a calculator in both exams.

There are a Few Golden Rules...

1) **Always, always, always make sure you read the question properly.**
   E.g. if you're asked about aerobic respiration, don't waffle on about anaerobic respiration.

2) **Look at the number of marks a question is worth.**
   The number of marks gives you a pretty good clue about how much to write. There's no point writing an essay for a question that's only worth one mark — it's just a waste of your time.

3) **Write your answers as clearly as you can.**
   If the examiner can't read your answer you won't get any marks, even if it's right.

4) **Use the correct terminology.**
   Using the right PE words shows you really know your stuff — so make sure you know your deviance from your gamesmanship, and your vasodilation from your vasoconstriction.

5) **Pay attention to the time.**
   If you're totally, hopelessly stuck on a question, just leave it and move on to the next one. You can always go back to it at the end if you've got enough time.

...and one extra tip for Extended Writing Questions

Each extended writing question in this book has a grey box around the question number.

1) Each paper will have two 9-mark extended writing questions. To get full marks on them, you need to show your PE knowledge about the topic in the question, apply it to the question context, and then make a judgement about what you're asked.

2) Don't panic if you think you can't do all that — you can still get a few marks just for doing some of it, so you might as well have a go.

You Need to Understand The Command Words

Command words are the words in a question that tell you what to do. If you don't know what they mean, you might not be able to answer the questions properly. Here are a few that crop up often:

Describe — You need to use your knowledge of PE facts to write about what something is like.

Define — Give the precise meaning of a word or phrase.

Explain — This means you should give reasons for something or say why or how something happens.

Assess — You need to write about how important or relevant something is in a certain context.

Analyse — Break something down into parts to show why or how something happens.

Justify — This means you need to give reasons for a choice.

Evaluate — Weigh up different factors in a debate or argument, then come to a judgement.

The Skeletal System

1 Which one of the following is classified as a flat bone? *(Grade 1-3)*

A   Humerus   ☐

B   Patella   ☐

C   Rib   ☐

D   Clavicle   ☐

[Total 1 mark]

2 Which one of the following is a ball and socket joint? *(Grade 1-3)*

A   Wrist   ☐

B   Knee   ☐

C   Elbow   ☐

D   Hip   ☐

[Total 1 mark]

3 Which one of the following is the name for the joint movement at the ankle when lifting the toes? *(Grade 1-3)*

A   Plantar-flexion   ☐

B   Dorsi-flexion   ☐

C   Circumduction   ☐

D   Adduction   ☐

[Total 1 mark]

4 State the types of joint movement that are possible at the elbow. *(Grade 1-3)*

....

....

[Total 1 mark]

4

5 Give **one** example of a sporting movement that uses abduction of the arm at the shoulder. *(Grade 3-5)*

....

[Total 1 mark]

6 Explain, using **one** example, how the cranium could protect a performer when taking part in sport. *(Grade 3-5)*

....

....

[Total 2 marks]

7 Explain the role of ligaments in the skeletal system. *(Grade 3-5)*

....

....

....

....

[Total 3 marks]

8 One function of the skeleton is muscle attachment. *(Grade 3-5)*

Explain how this function allows a performer to take part in physical activity.

....

....

....

....

[Total 2 marks]

9 **Figure 1** shows a footballer preparing to kick the ball.

Figure 1

Analyse, using **one** example, how **one** of the hinge joints in the footballer's body helps her to kick the ball.

For this question, you need to pick a hinge joint that the footballer is using, then say what movement it allows and how it helps to kick the ball.

....

....

....

....

....

....

....

[Total 3 marks]

10 Analyse the movements occurring at the hip joint when cycling.

....

....

....

....

[Total 2 marks]

Score: ⬜ **/17**

Exam Practice Tip

Most questions about the skeletal system won't just want you to state facts about the skeleton — they'll also want you to say how the skeleton's functions or features help you to perform well in physical activity and sport. That means you need to write about what bones, joints and connective tissues do — and write about their effects on performance as well.

Section One — Anatomy and Physiology

The Muscular System

1 The quadriceps are part of the body's muscular system. (Grade 1-3)

(a) State the main function of the quadriceps.

....

[1]

(b) Give **one** sporting example of a movement that uses the quadriceps.

....

[1]
[Total 2 marks]

2 **Figure 1** shows a basketball player taking a shot at the hoop. (Grade 5-7)

Position A   Position B

iStock.com/PhotoAttractive

Figure 1

Analyse the movement and muscle action at the elbow as the basketball player in **Figure 1** moves from position A to position B.

> You need to talk about what's happening in <u>both pictures</u> to get all the marks for this question.

....

....

....

....

....

....

....

[Total 4 marks]

3 Evaluate the importance of type I and type IIA muscle fibres for a marathon runner.

These 9-mark questions might look tricky, but don't panic — you can pick up the first few marks just by describing the muscle fibre types in the question. Make sure you also say when each type would be used during a marathon, and evaluate how important they are.

....

....

....

....

....

....

....

....

....

....

....

....

....

....

....

....

....

....

....

....

....

....

....

[Total 9 marks]

Score: ☐ /15

Section One — Anatomy and Physiology

The Cardiovascular System

1 Which one of the following carries deoxygenated blood towards the lungs? *(Grade 1-3)*

    A   Tricuspid valve   ☐

    B   Pulmonary vein   ☐

    C   Bicuspid valve   ☐

    D   Pulmonary artery   ☐

[Total 1 mark]

2 Which one of the following transports blood into the right atrium of the heart? *(Grade 1-3)*

    A   Vena cava   ☐

    B   Aorta   ☐

    C   Right ventricle   ☐

    D   Semi-lunar valve   ☐

[Total 1 mark]

3 State **two** functions of capillaries. *(Grade 1-3)*

1 ....

2 ....

[Total 2 marks]

4 Explain how the cardiovascular system controls temperature and how this aids performance in physical activity and sport. *(Grade 3-5)*

....

....

....

....

....

[Total 2 marks]

5 Explain **one** way that the structure of arteries makes them suited to their function. (Grade 3-5)

....

....

....

[Total 2 marks]

6 Blood can be redistributed around the body to meet the demands of physical activity. (Grade 5-7)

(a) Identify **two** areas of the body that would experience
an increase in blood flow when swimming.

1 ....

2 ....

[2]

(b) Explain your choices.

....

....

....

[3]
[Total 5 marks]

7 Assess the importance of the number of red blood cells to an endurance athlete. (Grade 7-9)

....

....

....

....

....

....

[Total 3 marks]

Score: [ ] / 16

Section One — Anatomy and Physiology

The Respiratory System

1 A performer's breathing changes during exercise. (Grade 1-3)

(a) Define **tidal volume** and **vital capacity**.

....

....

....

....

[2]

(b) State what happens to tidal volume during exercise.

....

....

[1]

[Total 3 marks]

2 Complete the following statements about the components of the respiratory system. (Grade 1-3)

Air flows through the mouth or nose into the ...., then into

the .... These then split into progressively smaller tubes called

...., which the air flows through to reach the alveoli.

[Total 3 marks]

3 Describe the action of the diaphragm when inhaling and exhaling. (Grade 3-5)

....

....

....

....

....

[Total 2 marks]

4 Explain the differences in composition between inhaled and exhaled air. (Grade 3-5)

....

....

....

....

....

....

[Total 4 marks]

5 Explain how the thin walls of alveoli assist them in their function. (Grade 5-7)

....

....

....

....

....

....

[Total 3 marks]

6 Assess the importance of a high vital capacity to a triathlete. (Grade 7-9)

....

....

....

....

....

....

[Total 3 marks]

Score: ⬚ **/18**

Section One — Anatomy and Physiology

Aerobic and Anaerobic Exercise

1 Which one of the following types of activity would be most likely to use fats as a fuel source?

(Grade 1-3)

A Anaerobic ☐

B Low intensity aerobic ☐

C Moderate intensity aerobic ☐

D Maximum intensity ☐

[Total 1 mark]

2 Evaluate the importance of aerobic and anaerobic respiration during a 50-mile cycling race.

Don't worry if you're not too sure where to start with this question — it's got a bit of the answer to give you a hand.

Aerobic respiration uses glucose and oxygen to release energy, and is needed for activities that

require endurance. It would be required for a 50-mile cycling race because...

....

....

....

....

....

....

....

....

....

....

....

....

....

....

....

....

[Total 9 marks]

Score: ☐ /10

Short-Term Effects of Exercise

1 Explain what is meant by the term **oxygen debt**. (Grade 1-3)

....

....

[Total 2 marks]

2 Explain why heart rate increases when a performer takes part in physical activity. (Grade 3-5)

....

....

....

....

....

[Total 3 marks]

3 Cardiac output is measured in litres per minute (l/min). A performer's cardiac output was calculated before, during and after a run on a treadmill. The values are shown in **Table 1**. (Grade 3-5)

| 5.53 l/min | 23.62 l/min | 10.34 l/min |

Table 1

(a) Identify from **Table 1** the cardiac output values recorded **during** and **after** the run.

....

....

[2]

(b) Give reasons for your answers.

....

....

....

....

[2]

[Total 4 marks]

14

4 **Figure 1** shows the heart rate of a performer during two 40-minute workouts on a cross trainer.

Grade 3-5

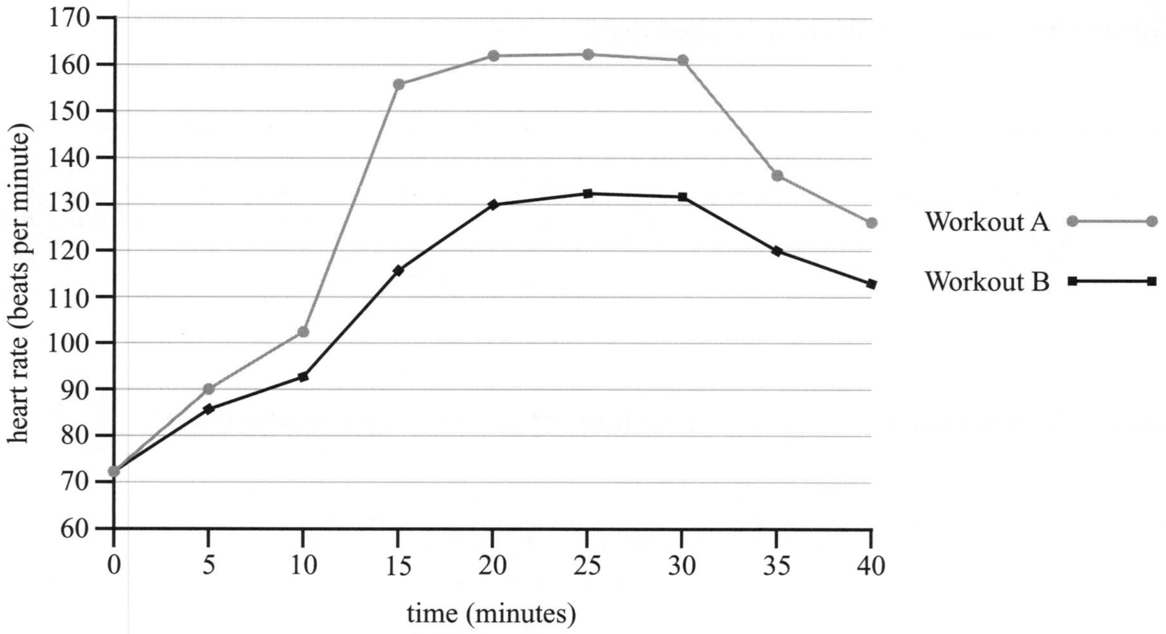

Figure 1

Analyse the heart rate data in **Figure 1** to explain what it suggests about the difference in intensity between the two workouts.

....

....

....

....

....

[Total 2 marks]

5 Assess the importance of increased tidal volume to a 100 m sprinter.

Grade 5-7

....

....

....

....

....

....

[Total 3 marks]

Score: ☐ /14

Long-Term Effects of Exercise

1 State **two** long-term training effects on the cardio-respiratory system. [Grade 1-3]

1 ....

2 ....

[Total 2 marks]

2 One long-term effect of exercise can be an increase in muscle girth. [Grade 5-7]

Explain, using **one** example, how this could benefit performance in physical activity and sport.

....

....

....

....

....

[Total 3 marks]

3 Hitesh has been training for a marathon for six months. During this time, he has noticed a decrease in his resting heart rate. [Grade 7-9]

Explain how Hitesh's marathon training will have led to a decrease in his resting heart rate.

Think about the effects on the heart during a marathon training session, and the effect this would have in the long term.

....

....

....

....

....

....

[Total 4 marks]

Score: [ ] /9

Exam Practice Tip

If an exam question asks you to explain how a long-term effect of exercise benefits someone's performance, make sure you give plenty of details. So as well as writing about the effects on the body's cardio-respiratory or musculo-skeletal systems, give examples of what they will help the performer to do — such as exercising more intensely or for longer.

Section One — Anatomy and Physiology

Lever Systems

1   **Figure 1** shows a diagram of a lever system. (Grade 1-3)

Figure 1

Complete the following statements about the components of the lever system in **Figure 1**.

The square is used to represent the .... of the lever system. The arrow

represents the .... and the triangle represents the ....

[Total 3 marks]

2   When kicking a football, a lever system operates to move the knee joint from flexion to extension. (Grade 5-7)

Identify the load, fulcrum and effort in this lever system.

....

....

[Total 3 marks]

3   A gymnast uses the body's lever systems to stand on their toes.

(a) Classify the lever operating at the ankle as the gymnast stands on their toes. (Grade 5-7)

....

[1]

(b) Analyse how the lever operating at the ankle assists the gymnast when standing on their toes. (Grade 7-9)

> Think about the benefits of the lever class you gave in part (a), and how they would help someone to stand on their toes.

....

....

....

....

....

....

[3]

[Total 4 marks]

Score: ☐ / **10**

Planes and Axes of Movement

1 Which one of the following is the name of the movement plane that divides the body into left and right sides? *(Grade 1-3)*

    A   Vertical ☐

    B   Transverse ☐

    C   Frontal ☐

    D   Sagittal ☐

[Total 1 mark]

2 Which one of the following is the name of the axis that runs through the body from top to bottom? *(Grade 1-3)*

    A   Sagittal ☐

    B   Transverse ☐

    C   Frontal ☐

    D   Vertical ☐

[Total 1 mark]

3 State the plane and axis used during the following movements.

(i) Cartwheel *(Grade 3-5)*

....

....

[2]

(ii) Forward roll *(Grade 5-7)*

....

....

[2]

(iii) Ice skating spin *(Grade 5-7)*

....

....

[2]

[Total 6 marks]

Score: ☐ /**8**

⌢ ☐   ⌣ ☐   ☺ ☐

Section Three — Physical Training

Health and Fitness

1 Which one of the following is a definition of **fitness**? (Grade 1-3)

   A   Fitness is the ability to use two or more parts
       of the body together, efficiently and accurately ☐

   B   Fitness is exercising for at least 150 minutes every week ☐

   C   Having a high level of fitness means you are physically healthy ☐

   D   Having a high level of fitness means you can meet the demands of your environment ☐

   [Total 1 mark]

2 Christine trains regularly. She has achieved a high level of fitness with her training programme.

   (a) Define the term **health**. (Grade 1-3)

   ....

   ....

   [1]

   (b) Explain why Christine might not be classed as healthy, despite her high level of fitness. (Grade 5-7)

   ....

   ....

   ....

   [2]

   [Total 3 marks]

3 Explain the roles of exercise, fitness and health in the performance of a sportsperson. (Grade 5-7)

   ....

   ....

   ....

   ....

   ....

   ....

   ....

   [Total 4 marks]

   Score: ☐ /**8**

☹ ☐   ☺ ☐   ☺ ☐

Components of Fitness

1 Which of these stages of a 100 m sprint event requires a short reaction time? *Grade 1-3*

    A During the warm-up ☐

    B At the start of the race, when the starter pistol is fired ☐

    C While accelerating away from the starting blocks ☐

    D During recovery, after the race is finished ☐

[Total 1 mark]

2 Which of the following components of fitness is the **least** important for a marathon runner? *Grade 1-3*

    A Body Composition ☐

    B Cardiovascular Fitness ☐

    C Agility ☐

    D Muscular Endurance ☐

[Total 1 mark]

3 Complete the following definition of **body composition**. *Grade 1-3*

Body composition is the percentage of .... made up by

.... , muscle and bone.

[Total 2 marks]

4 Balance is a component of fitness. *Grade 1-3*

(a) Give a definition of **balance**.

....

[1]

(b) Give **one** example of when a gymnast would need good balance.

....

....

[1]

[Total 2 marks]

5 Shinji wants to improve his performance in squash.
He finds that his arms get tired towards the end of a match. (Grade 3-5)

Identify the component of fitness Shinji should improve to address the tiredness in his arms.

....

[Total 1 mark]

6 Explain why coordination is important for a tennis player. (Grade 3-5)

....

....

....

....

[Total 2 marks]

7 Ben is training to compete in the shot-put and has been working on his strength.

(a) Identify **two** more components of fitness besides strength (Grade 3-5)
that Ben should focus on improving in training.

Component 1 ....

Component 2 ....

[2]

(b) Justify your choices by explaining how improving these components of fitness (Grade 5-7)
would affect his performance in the shot-put.

Justification for component 1

....

....

Justification for component 2

....

....

[2]

[Total 4 marks]

Exam Practice Tip

In questions about components of fitness you won't get all the marks by saying something vague — like 'reaction time helps in football'. Instead, you need to give specific sporting actions that components of fitness are involved in — so write something like 'a short reaction time helps football players respond quickly to a pass' to get all those lovely marks.

Section Three — Physical Training

8 Explain how improving flexibility can help improve a golfer's performance. (Grade 5-7)

....

....

....

....

....

[Total 3 marks]

9 Jamie is a hockey player. Roberta is a 100 m sprinter.

(a) Give a definition of the term **agility**. (Grade 1-3)

....

[1]

(b) Explain whether agility is more important to Jamie or Roberta in helping them to perform well in their sport. (Grade 5-7)

....

....

....

[3]

[Total 4 marks]

10 Cardiovascular fitness and power are components of fitness. (Grade 7-9)

Assess the relative importance of these components of fitness for a long jumper.

Often, there's more than one point you could make about how components of fitness are used by a performer. E.g. instead of what's already written in part (i) below, you could say that cardiovascular fitness is needed for long training sessions...

(i) Cardiovascular fitness

Good cardiovascular fitness means you can exercise the whole body for a long time. A long jumper only has to run for a short amount of time, so...

....

....

[3]

(ii) Power

....

....

....

....

[3]

[Total 6 marks]

Section Three — Physical Training

11 Lizzy is a gymnast and Anita is a footballer.

(a) State whether Lizzy or Anita will require more flexibility to perform well. (Grade 3-5)

....

[1]

(b) Explain your answer to part (a) using examples of sporting (Grade 5-7) actions from gymnastics and football.

....

....

....

[2]

[Total 3 marks]

12 Evaluate whether cardiovascular fitness or strength is more important for an Olympic weightlifter.

This nine mark question might look a bit scary, but it's not too bad if you break it down into smaller chunks. Here's an example of how you could show your knowledge of cardiovascular fitness and apply it to the performer...

Good cardiovascular fitness means the heart and lungs can supply the muscles with oxygen so the whole body can be exercised for a long time. As weightlifting is a short duration, anaerobic event, cardiovascular fitness would not directly help the weightlifter to compete. However, it would mean the weightlifter could train for longer, and recover in a shorter time, which would help them to perform well.

Now you need to do something similar for strength...

....

....

....

....

....

....

....

....

....

And don't forget to write a conclusion at the end...

....

....

....

[Total 9 marks]

Score: ☐ **/38**

Fitness Testing

1   Which of the following components of fitness does the vertical jump test measure? *(Grade 1-3)*

A   Power ☐

B   Speed ☐

C   Muscular endurance ☐

D   Strength ☐

[Total 1 mark]

2   Which one of the following fitness tests measures flexibility? *(Grade 1-3)*

A   Grip dynamometer test ☐

B   Sit and reach test ☐

C   30 m sprint test ☐

D   Harvard step test ☐

[Total 1 mark]

3   The one-minute sit-up test is a fitness test for muscular endurance. *(Grade 1-3)*

Describe how to carry out the one-minute sit-up test and say what the result tells you.

....

....

....

....

[Total 2 marks]

4   Salima is a rock climber who wants to improve how firmly she can hold onto a rock face. *(Grade 3-5)*

State a fitness test she could use to monitor her progress.

....

[Total 1 mark]

Section Three — Physical Training

24

5 Eric is planning a personal exercise programme (PEP).

(a) Describe **two** ways that Eric can use fitness testing to help him plan and carry out his PEP. (Grade 3-5)

1 ....

....

2 ....

....

[2]

Eric is training to compete in a triathlon.

(b) Explain why the Cooper 12-minute run test might be more useful (Grade 5-7) to him than the 30 m sprint test.

....

....

....

[3]

After six weeks of training, Eric finds that the distance he manages to run on the Cooper 12-minute run test has not increased.

(c) State what this tells Eric about the effectiveness of his training programme. (Grade 3-5)

....

[1]

[Total 6 marks]

6 Assess the relative importance of the sit and reach test and the Illinois agility run test for a footballer. (Grade 7-9)

Think about which component of fitness each of these tests measures.

(i) Sit and reach test

....

....

....

[3]

(ii) Illinois agility run test

....

....

....

[3]

[Total 6 marks]

Score: ☐ /**17**

Section Three — Physical Training

☺☐ ☺☐ ☺☐

Fitness Testing — Data Questions

1   **Table 1** shows ratings for the grip dynamometer test for people aged 16-19 years old.

Gender	Excellent	Good	Average	Fair	Poor
Male	>56 kg	51-56 kg	45-50 kg	39-44 kg	<39 kg
Female	>36 kg	31-36 kg	25-30 kg	19-24 kg	<19 kg

Table 1

Gabrielle is 17. She took the grip dynamometer test and scored 33 kg.

Select the correct rating for Gabrielle.

A   Good   ☐

B   Average   ☐

C   Fair   ☐

D   Poor   ☐

Make sure you check the right row of the table.

[Total 1 mark]

2   Angus is 16. Using **Table 1**, give a score he could get on the grip dynamometer test to be classified as having **good** grip strength.

....

[Total 1 mark]

3   Amir has been following a training programme.

Table 2 shows the results of two different fitness tests that Amir has done in each week of his training programme.

Fitness Test	Week					
	1	2	3	4	5	6
Sit and reach test (cm)	5.0	5.0	5.5	6.0	6.5	7.0
One minute sit-up test (no. of sit-ups)	25	25	24	25	24	25

Table 2

(a) Analyse the data in **Table 2** and describe the trends for each of the fitness tests.

....

....

....

[2]

(b) Using the data in **Table 2**, identify **one** component of fitness that Amir's training is improving.

....

[1]

[Total 3 marks]

Score: ☐ **/5**

Principles of Training

1 Give **three** methods of achieving overload in training. (Grade 1-3)

1 ....

....

2 ....

....

3 ....

....

[Total 3 marks]

2 Lucy is planning a training programme to prepare herself for taking part in a marathon. (Grade 3-5)

(a) Using an example, explain how Lucy could use the principle of progressive overload in her training.

....

....

....

....

....

[2]

(b) Specificity is another principle of training.
   (i) Define **specificity**.

....

....

[1]

(ii) Give **one** example of how Lucy could apply specificity to her training.

....

....

....

[1]

[Total 4 marks]

3 Ele is a GCSE student carrying out a personal exercise programme (PEP). She suffers an injury and is unable to train for four weeks.

Ele's cardiovascular fitness had been improving with her training.

(a) Explain how Ele may be affected by reversibility during the four weeks.

....

....

....

[2]

Ele's coach thinks that she might have been injured because she was overtraining.

(b) Explain how Ele could avoid overtraining in the future.

....

....

[2]

[Total 4 marks]

4 Jeffrey is a rock climber. Evaluate whether the use of the training principles individual needs, specificity and progressive overload in Jeffrey's training could help him to avoid injury.

Another one of those tricky nine-markers here. The answer has already been started for you — finish it by writing something covering the other two principles, then wrapping it all up with a conclusion....

Using the principle of individual needs, Jeffrey will plan a training programme that is tailored to him personally. This means his level of training will be suitable for his age and his level of fitness and skill, so he will not attempt to climb anything he is not ready for. This will help Jeffrey to avoid injury by making sure he is not overworking his body.

....

....

....

....

....

....

....

....

Your conclusion will need to compare the three principles and how they help Jeffrey avoid injury...

....

[Total 9 marks]

Score: _____ **/20**

Section Three — Physical Training

Training Target Zones

1 Fatima is training for a weightlifting competition. State whether Fatima should spend more of her time training aerobically or anaerobically. Justify your answer.

(Grade 3-5)

....

....

....

[Total 2 marks]

2 Leonardo is 25 years old. (Grade 5-7)

Remember, to work out target zones, first work out the maximum heart rate.

(a) Calculate the lower threshold of his aerobic target zone.

....

....

....

....

[3]

Figure 1 shows Leonardo's heart rate while he was running on a treadmill, measured in each week of his training.

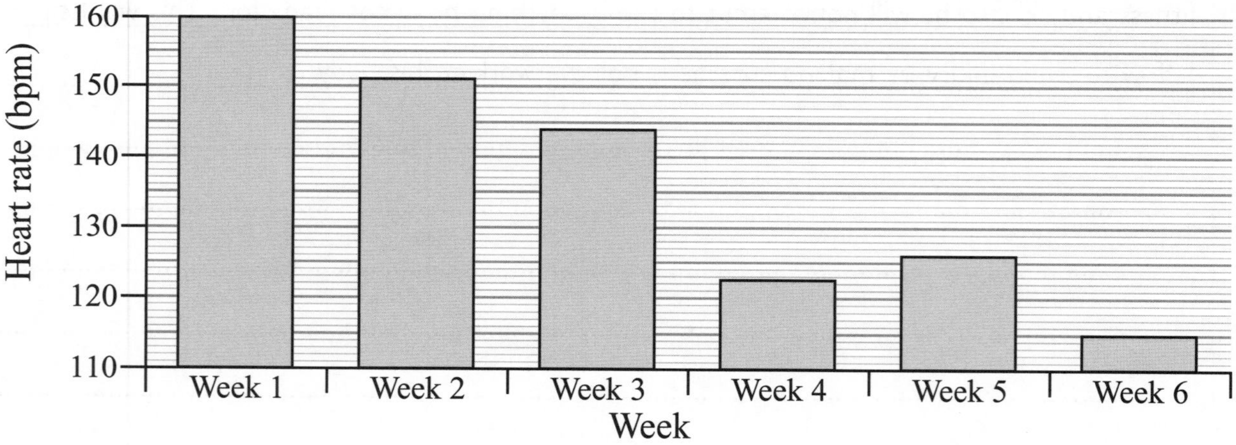

Figure 1

(b) State the weeks in which Leonardo was working within his aerobic target zone.

....

....

[2]

[Total 5 marks]

Score: [   ] **/7**

Training Methods

1 Which of the following statements best describes Fartlek training? *(Grade 1-3)*

    A   Training at a constant rate and intensity ☐

    B   Combining high intensity work with rest periods ☐

    C   A type of continuous training that involves changes in intensity ☐

    D   A type of training that develops strength ☐

[Total 1 mark]

2 Give **three** ways that overload can be achieved in continuous training. *(Grade 1-3)*

1 ....

2 ....

3 ....

[Total 3 marks]

3 Complete the following statement about resistance training. *(Grade 1-3)*

Resistance training can be used to improve strength, power and ....

To improve strength, a .... weight is used, with a .... number of reps.

[Total 3 marks]

4 Lesley has just started playing basketball. *(Grade 3-5)*

Identify **two** methods of training she could use to improve her performance.
Justify each choice.

Method 1 ....

....

Method 2 ....

....

[Total 4 marks]

5   Complete the following table about two training methods, one component of fitness each method improves and one long-term adaptation to the body each method can cause.

Training method	Component of fitness improved	Long-term training adaptation to body systems
....	Strength	....
Continuous	....	....

[Total 4 marks]

6   N'Golo wants to improve his cardiovascular fitness and his leg strength.

He decides to use circuit training.

(a) Give **one** advantage and **one** disadvantage of circuit training. (Grade 1-3)

Advantage

....

....

Disadvantage

....

....

[2]

(b) State **one** circuit station N'Golo could use to improve his: (Grade 3-5)

(i) Cardiovascular fitness

....

[1]

(ii) Leg strength

....

[1]

(c) Identify **one** fitness class that N'Golo could attend to help him achieve his fitness goals. (Grade 3-5) Justify your answer.

....

....

....

[2]

[Total 6 marks]

Section Three — Physical Training

7 **Figure 1** shows the heart rate of an athlete during a period of their training.

Grade 7-9

Time (minutes)

Figure 1

Analyse the graph and state **one** method of training the athlete could be using. Justify your answer.

....

....

[Total 2 marks]

8 Evaluate the use of interval training and continuous training by a basketball player.

Another nine-marker here, and the answer's already been started for you — how nice...

Continuous training involves training at a constant rate, without any rests. It improves

cardiovascular fitness, which will help the basketball player to use their muscles continuously

throughout a game.

....

....

....

....

....

....

....

....

Remember to mention both types of training in your conclusion.

....

....

[Total 9 marks]

Score: ⬚/**32**

Exam Practice Tip

For training questions like the one above, you don't have to stick to just talking about the methods of training named in the question. If there's another method that's relevant to the performer in the question, don't be afraid to mention it.

Section Three — Physical Training

Preventing Injuries

1 Describe what a PARQ is and when it would be used. (Grade 1-3)

....

....

....

[Total 2 marks]

2 State **three** stages of a warm-up. (Grade 1-3)

1 ....

2 ....

3 ....

[Total 3 marks]

3 Mrs Costanza is a PE teacher. She has started an after school hockey club. She always makes sure that students warm up before playing, and cool down afterwards.

(a) State **three** more actions she can take to reduce the risk of injury to students during hockey club. (Grade 3-5)

1 ....

2 ....

3 ....

[3]

(b) Explain how **two** of the actions listed above can reduce the risk of injury for hockey players. (Grade 5-7)

1 ....

....

....

2 ....

....

....

[4]

[Total 7 marks]

Score: ☐ /12

Injuries and Treatment

1 Which of the following is **not** a soft-tissue injury? *(Grade 1-3)*

A Stress fracture ☐

B Sprain ☐

C Abrasion ☐

D Tennis elbow ☐

[Total 1 mark]

2 Complete **Table 1** to show the types of tissue damaged in different injuries. *(Grade 1-3)*

Injury	Damaged Tissue
Sprain	....
Strain	....
Golfer's Elbow	....

Table 1

[Total 3 marks]

3 **Table 2** shows two types of fracture. *(Grade 3-5)*

Complete **Table 2** by writing the performers **A** and **B** next to the type of fracture they are most likely to suffer from while taking part in their activity.

A 45-year-old marathon runner   **B** 22-year-old rugby player

Type of fracture	Performer
Stress	....
Compound	....

Table 2

[Total 2 marks]

4 Riyad is a footballer and Danielle is a long distance runner. *(Grade 3-5)*

State whether Riyad or Danielle is more likely to suffer a concussion taking part in their sport. Justify your answer.

....

....

....

....

[Total 3 marks]

5 RICE is a method of treating injury.

(a) State what the R and the C in RICE stand for. (Grade 1-3)

R ....

C ....

[2]

(b) The I in RICE stands for ice.
Explain how applying ice helps to treat an injury. (Grade 5-7)

....

....

[2]

[Total 4 marks]

6 **Figure 2** shows two rugby players during a tackle. (Grade 5-7)

Identify **two** types of soft-tissue injury that one of the players could receive and explain how each might occur.

Figure 2

1 ....

....

....

[2]

2 ....

....

....

[2]

[Total 4 marks]

Score: ☐ /**17**

Exam Practice Tip

To answer exam questions about injuries, you will need to know which types of injuries are more likely in different types of sports. Injuries that are caused by a sudden impact will be more likely in sports where there is contact between performers. Sprains are common in sports where players often change direction, or which involve lots of jumping.

😐 ☐   🙂 ☐   😊 ☐

Performance-Enhancing Drugs

1   Which one of the following statements about performance-enhancing drugs and their effects is **true**?   (Grade 1-3)

    A   Anabolic steroids kill pain, which helps athletes to train despite being injured   ☐

    B   Stimulants increase the amount you urinate, which causes weight loss   ☐

    C   Narcotic analgesics act in a similar way to the hormone testosterone, so increase bone and muscle growth   ☐

    D   Beta Blockers lower the heart rate and have a calming, relaxing effect   ☐

[Total 1 mark]

2   Give **one** performance benefit and **one** negative side-effect of stimulants.   (Grade 3-5)

....

....

[Total 2 marks]

3   State whether beta blockers or anabolic steroids would bring the greater performance gains for a shot-putter. Justify your answer.   (Grade 3-5)

....

....

[Total 2 marks]

4   Erythropoietin (EPO) comes under the classification of peptide hormones.

    (a)   State **two** possible side effects of EPO.   (Grade 1-3)

      1 ....

      2 ....

[2]

    (b)   Explain how EPO could improve an endurance athlete's performance.   (Grade 5-7)

....

....

....

[3]

[Total 5 marks]

Score: ☐ / **10**

Exam Practice Tip

Performance-enhancing drugs are illegal and have some nasty side effects — unfortunately some people still choose to use them... If you're asked to work out which drug would give the greatest performance benefits for a certain sportsperson, a good tactic is to narrow down your options by working backwards to eliminate the ones that obviously don't apply.

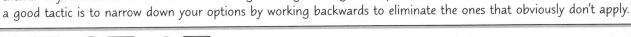

Health, Fitness and Well-being

1   Which of the following is an emotional benefit of exercise? (Grade 1-3)

    A   Regular exercise makes you stronger and more flexible ☐

    B   Regular exercise helps you maintain a healthy weight ☐

    C   Regular exercise improves your cardiovascular system ☐

    D   Regular exercise can help to increase self-esteem ☐

[Total 1 mark]

2   Complete the following statement about the effect of exercise on the brain. (Grade 1-3)

Exercise increases the level of endorphins and .... in your brain,

which may make you feel happier and help to reduce the risk of depression.

[Total 1 mark]

3   Khalid has just started a new job and is finding that he is feeling more stressed than he used to. A friend suggests that doing regular exercise may help.

(a) Explain how regular exercise could help Khalid. (Grade 3-5)

....

....

[2]

(b) State **two** ways exercise could help Khalid's social well-being. (Grade 1-3)

1 ....

....

2 ....

....

[2]

[Total 4 marks]

4 Complete the following statement about osteoporosis. (Grade 1-3)

Osteoporosis is a disease that causes .... to become weak and fragile.

Doing regular .... exercise can help to prevent osteoporosis.

[Total 2 marks]

5 Explain how exercise can lead to an increase in someone's self-esteem. (Grade 3-5)

....

....

....

....

[Total 2 marks]

6 Regular exercise can help to prevent osteoporosis and type-2 diabetes. (Grade 5-7)

(a) Explain how regular exercise can help to reduce **one** other long-term physical health risk.

....

....

....

....

....

[3]

(b) Explain **one** way in which exercise can have a negative effect on physical well-being.

....

....

....

[2]

[Total 5 marks]

Score: ☐ /**15**

Exam Practice Tip

If you need to figure out whether a benefit of exercise is physical, emotional or social, try to think about which part of your life it affects. If it affects your body's systems (apart from your brain), it's probably physical. If it affects your feelings or your brain, then it's emotional. If it involves your relationships with other people, then it's social.

 ☐ ☐ ☐ Section Four — Health, Fitness and Well-being

Lifestyle Choices

1 Which of the following describes the effect of nicotine on the body? (Grade 1-3)

   A It raises heart rate and blood pressure ☐

   B It damages cilia, leading to a higher risk of infection ☐

   C It damages alveoli, causing emphysema ☐

   D It increases the risk of pneumonia ☐

   [Total 1 mark]

2 Explain how being under the influence of alcohol could affect performance in a physical activity or sport. (Grade 3-5)

....

....

....

   [Total 2 marks]

3 Assess the impact of lack of sleep on performance in gymnastics. (Grade 5-7)

....

....

....

....

....

   [Total 3 marks]

Score: ☐ / 6

Exam Practice Tip

Remember to use connecting words like 'and', 'but', 'however', 'because' and 'therefore' when you answer longer questions. If you link your sentences together, <u>then</u> the examiner will whoop with joy. This is good, <u>because</u> a chuffed examiner means plenty of marks. <u>Therefore</u>, by using connecting words, you will ace your exam <u>and</u> be happy for evermore...

   ☐ ☺ ☐ ☐

Sedentary Lifestyle

1 Being overweight means weighing more than is normal.

(a) State **one** possible effect of being overweight on the cardiovascular system. (Grade 1-3)

....

[1]

(b) Explain, using **one** example, how being overweight could impact performance in physical activity and sport. (Grade 3-5)

....

....

....

[2]

[Total 3 marks]

2 A sedentary lifestyle can lead to a wide range of health problems.

(a) Define a **sedentary lifestyle**. (Grade 1-3)

....

....

[1]

(b) State **two** possible long-term effects of a sedentary lifestyle on the musculo-skeletal system. (Grade 3-5)

1 ....

2 ....

[2]

(c) Explain how exercise can help to prevent the long-term effects described in (b). (Grade 5-7)

1 ....

....

....

2 ....

....

....

[4]

[Total 7 marks]

Score: .... / **10**

Section Four — Health, Fitness and Well-being

Physical Health — Data Questions

1   **Figure 1** shows the proportion of smokers in Great Britain from 1974 to 2012.

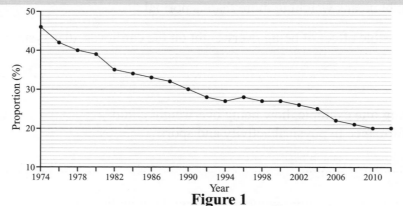

Figure 1

(a) State the proportion of people who smoked in 2002. Grade 1-3

....

[1]

(b) Analyse **Figure 1** and state the trend shown. Grade 3-5

....

[1]
[Total 2 marks]

2   **Figure 2** shows the percentage of adults that were obese by gender from 1993 to 2013. Grade 5-7

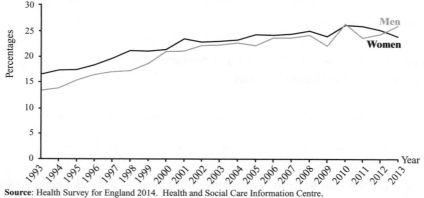

Source: Health Survey for England 2014. Health and Social Care Information Centre.

Figure 2

Analyse **Figure 2**.

(a) State the overall trend in the obesity of adults shown by the data.

....

[1]

(b) Describe the changes in obesity rates for men and women between 2009 and 2013.

....

....

....

[4]
[Total 5 marks]

Score: ☐ /7

Diet, Nutrition and Performance

1 Which one of the following is the recommended balance of macronutrients in the diet of an average person? *Grade 1-3*

    A   50-55% carbohydrates, 35-40% fats, 10-15% proteins ☐

    B   55-60% carbohydrates, 25-30% fats, 15-20% proteins ☐

    C   55-60% carbohydrates, 35-40% fats, 5-10% proteins ☐

    D   40-45% carbohydrates, 25-30% fats, 30-25% proteins ☐

[Total 1 mark]

2 Which of the following nutrients helps to maintain strong bones and teeth? *Grade 1-3*

    A   Minerals ☐

    B   Fibre ☐

    C   Fats ☐

    D   Carbohydrates ☐

[Total 1 mark]

3 Complete the table below describing the roles of different macronutrients. *Grade 1-3*

Macronutrient	Role in a balanced diet
....	Energy for low-intensity exercise
....	Repairing muscle
Carbohydrates	....

[Total 3 marks]

4 Maintaining hydration during sport is very important.

(a) State **two** consequences of dehydration. (Grade 1-3)

1 ....

2 ....

[2]

(b) Give **one** example of an activity where performers are at a high risk of dehydration. (Grade 5-7) Explain your answer.

....

....

[2]

[Total 4 marks]

5 Explain how timing of protein intake could improve performance in **one** physical activity or sport. (Grade 5-7)

....

....

....

....

....

[Total 4 marks]

6 **Figure 1** shows the proportions of different nutrients in a performer's diet. (Grade 7-9)

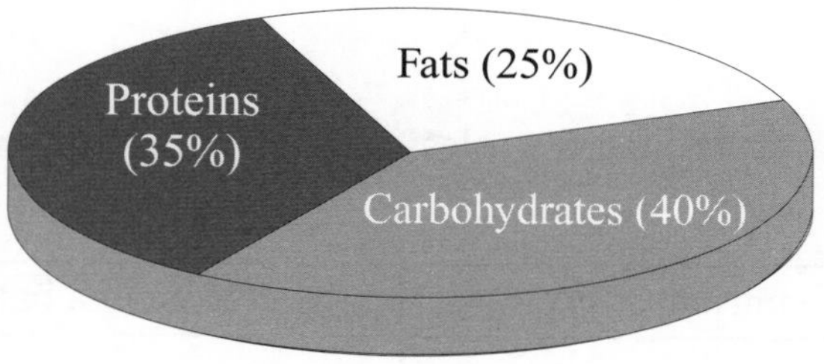

Fats (25%)
Proteins (35%)
Carbohydrates (40%)

Figure 1

You'll need to compare the percentages in the pie chart to the percentages an average person should eat, then think about what kind of performer might choose this diet.

Analyse **Figure 1** to suggest whether it is most likely to represent the diet of a marathon runner, shot-putter or long-distance cyclist. Justify your answer.

....

....

....

....

....

[Total 4 marks]

7 Evaluate the importance of carbohydrates and fats for performance in a marathon.

For this question, think about the various roles carbohydrates and fats play in physical activity.

....

....

....

....

....

....

....

....

....

....

....

....

....

....

....

....

....

....

....

Don't forget to come to some sort of conclusion comparing the importance of fats and carbohydrates.

....

....

[Total 9 marks]

Score: ☐ **/ 26**

Exam Practice Tip

There will be two of these nine-mark questions in your exam — that's 18 whole marks. They'll come at the end of the paper, so make sure you leave yourself enough time to have a good crack at them. It might even be worth skipping ahead and doing them early on in the exam, then going back and working your way through the rest of the paper.

 ☐ ☐ ☐

Section Four — Health, Fitness and Well-being

Optimum Weight

1   Which of the following statements about optimum weight is the most accurate? (Grade 1-3)

   A   An athlete's optimum weight is affected by the amount of carbohydrate in their diet ☐

   B   An athlete needs a balanced diet to achieve their optimum weight ☐

   C   Optimum weight is affected by bone structure, muscle girth, gender and height ☐

   D   The optimum weight for two performers in the same sport is always identical ☐

[Total 1 mark]

2   Complete the following statement about energy balance. (Grade 1-3)

   Weight gain occurs when more energy is taken in than is used up by the body — this is known as

   a .... energy balance. To lose weight, more energy must be used up than is

   taken in — this is known as a .... energy balance.

[Total 2 marks]

3   **Figure 1** shows performers in gymnastics and judo.

Figure 1

   (a) State which of the sports in **Figure 1** will require the higher optimum weight. (Grade 3-5)

   ....

[1]

   (b) Explain your answer to part (a), using examples (Grade 5-7) of sporting actions from gymnastics and judo.

   ....

   ....

   ....

[2]

[Total 3 marks]

Score: ☐ / 6

Skills and Practice

1 Explain the benefits of mental rehearsal for performance in physical activity and sport. (Grade 1-3)

....

....

[Total 2 marks]

2 Define the term **high organisation skill**. (Grade 1-3)

....

....

[Total 1 mark]

3 Sports skills can be classified using the open-closed continuum. An example is shown below. (Grade 5-7)

High jump

Closed ⊢————————×————————————————⊣ Open

Explain why the high jump may have been placed at this point on the continuum.

....

....

....

....

[Total 3 marks]

4 Assess the use of distributed practice for improving a somersault. (Grade 7-9)

Think about the type of skill that a somersault is.

....

....

....

....

[Total 3 marks]

Score: .... / **9**

Goal Setting

1 'SMART' stands for the five principles of goal setting. **(Grade 1-3)**

Describe the principle that 'S' represents.

....

....

[Total 1 mark]

2 'Measurable' is one of the principles of goal setting.

(a) Explain how this principle can be used to improve sports performance. **(Grade 3-5)**

....

....

....

....

[3]

Layla sets herself a goal to run 5 km in 27 minutes.

(b) Identify how this goal applies the 'measurable' principle of goal setting. **(Grade 3-5)**

....

....

....

[1]

(c) Explain how Layla could apply **two** other principles of goal setting to make her goal more effective. **(Grade 5-7)**

....

....

....

....

[4]

[Total 8 marks]

Score: ☐ /**9**

Exam Practice Tip

Goal setting questions tend to ask you how setting a goal or applying a principle of 'SMART' will help to improve performance in sport. So to make sure you get all the marks for this type of question, write about what effect the goal or principle will have on how the performer feels, then say how and why that effect will improve their performance.

Section Five — Sport Psychology

Guidance and Feedback

1 Define the term **mechanical guidance**. (Grade 1-3)

....

[Total 1 mark]

2 Describe the difference between concurrent and terminal feedback. (Grade 1-3)

....

....

[Total 2 marks]

3 Explain why extrinsic feedback is important to a beginner. (Grade 3-5)

....

....

....

[Total 3 marks]

4 A coach might use verbal and mechanical guidance to teach sporting skills. (Grade 7-9)

Assess the relative importance of these guidance types
when teaching a group of beginners how to swim.

(i) Verbal guidance

....

....

....

....

[3]

(ii) Mechanical guidance

....

....

....

....

[3]

[Total 6 marks]

Score: ☐ / **12**

Influences on Participation

1   Which one of the following is a socio-economic influence on whether someone participates in sport?   *(Grade 1-3)*

    A   Sexism   ☐

    B   Religious beliefs   ☐

    C   Cost   ☐

    D   Racism   ☐

[Total 1 mark]

2   Explain, using **one** example, how age can affect the level of participation in a sport.   *(Grade 3-5)*

....

....

....

....

[Total 3 marks]

3   Studies show that participation rates in physical activity and sport are lower for disabled people than they are for non-disabled people.   *(Grade 3-5)*

Give **two** possible reasons for the lower participation rates amongst disabled people.

1 ....

....

2 ....

....

[Total 2 marks]

4   Assess the importance of media coverage of women's sports for participation rates amongst women.   *(Grade 7-9)*

....

....

....

....

....

[Total 3 marks]

Score: ☐ /9

Participation Rates — Data Questions

1   Figure 1 shows participation rates for three activities in England.

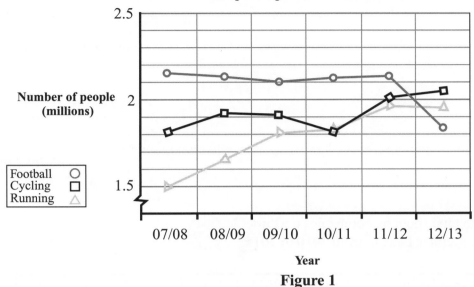

Graph showing the number of English people aged
16 or over who participated at least once a week.

Figure 1

Using the data in **Figure 1**, select the statement below that is true.

A   Participation rates in football, cycling and running increased from 07/08 to 12/13   ☐

B   In 12/13, more people participated in football than in running   ☐

C   Between 07/08 and 11/12, football was more popular than cycling or running   ☐

D   In 08/09, cycling was the least popular sport   ☐

[Total 1 mark]

2   Analyse the data in **Figure 1**.

(a) Identify the sport that saw the greatest increase in participation from 07/08 to 12/13. (Grade 3-5)

....

[1]

(b) Explain what you think will happen to the participation rate in cycling in 13/14. (Grade 7-9)

....

....

....

[2]

[Total 3 marks]

Score: ☐ / 4

 ☐   ☐   ☐   Section Six — Sport, Society and Culture

Commercialisation of Sport

1   Give **one** advantage and **one** disadvantage of sponsorship for sport as a whole.   Grade 3-5

Advantage

....

....

Disadvantage

....

....

[Total 2 marks]

2   **Figure 1** shows the total spent by companies on shirt   Grade 3-5
sponsorship in the Premier League from 2010 to 2015.

Year season began	2010	2011	2012	2013	2014	2015
Total spent (millions of pounds)	100.45	117.5	147.1	165.75	191.35	222.9

Figure 1

(a) Analyse **Figure 1**. State the first year in which spending
on shirt sponsorship was more than £150 million.

....

[1]

(b) Using **Figure 1**, calculate the increase in the total spent by companies
on shirt sponsorship in the Premier League from 2010 to 2015.

....

....

[1]

[Total 2 marks]

3   Explain how increased media coverage of the Paralympics   Grade 5-7
could affect sponsorship of the athletes involved.

....

....

....

....

[Total 3 marks]

4 Evaluate whether the increased commercialisation of sport has had a positive impact on players and performers.

It's another one of those tricky nine-markers... With this question, you need to make sure you weigh up the good and bad sides of the commercialisation of sport for players and performers.

....

....

....

....

....

....

....

....

....

....

....

....

....

....

....

....

....

....

....

....

....

....

....

[Total 9 marks]

Score: ☐ /16

Section Six — Sport, Society and Culture

Sporting Behaviour

1 Which one of the following is an example of deviance? (Grade 1-3)

    A   Trying to distract an opponent by grunting or shrieking in tennis ☐

    B   Timing the intake of protein to maximise muscle growth ☐

    C   Time-wasting in football ☐

    D   Deliberately tripping a player as they run down the pitch in hockey ☐

[Total 1 mark]

2 Most sports players display sportsmanship. (Grade 1-3)

    (a) Define **sportsmanship**.

    ....

    ....

    ....

[1]

    (b) Give **one** example of sportsmanship in a sport of your choice.

    ....

    ....

    ....

[1]

[Total 2 marks]

3 Discuss whether you would expect to see higher levels of deviance amongst professional athletes or amateurs. (Grade 7-9)

....

....

....

....

....

....

[Total 4 marks]

Score: ☐ /7

Exam Practice Tip

When you are asked to describe or define something, make sure you have a look at the number of marks available for the question — it'll give you a clue about how many points you need to make. Also, make sure to include plenty of detail in your answer — that way, you'll make it nice and obvious to the examiner how clever you are.

Sporting Behaviour — Data Questions

1   **Table 1** shows the numbers of yellow cards awarded each year at a five-a-side football tournament.

Year	2009	2010	2011	2012	2013	2014	2015
No. of yellow cards	6	7	10	11	8	9	12

Table 1

(a) Complete the graph below to display the data in **Table 1**.
Label the axes and join up the points to make a line graph. (Grade 3-5)

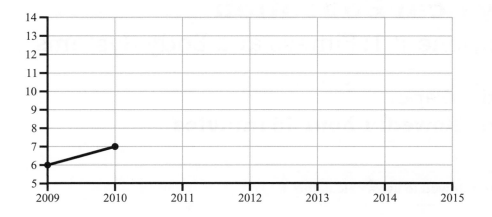

[2]

From 2013 the organisers of the tournament brought in a fine for anyone receiving a yellow card, to try to encourage fair play.

(b) Analyse the data in **Table 1** to determine whether the fine has been successful. Justify your answer. (Grade 5-7)

....

....

....

[2]

(c) Analyse the data in **Table 1** to predict whether the number of yellow cards awarded in 2016 (Grade 5-7) will be an increase or decrease on the number awarded in 2015. Justify your prediction.

....

....

[2]

[Total 6 marks]

Score: ☐ / **6**

 ☐   ☐   ☐

Candidate Surname		Candidate Forename(s)	

Centre Number	Candidate Number	Candidate Signature

GCSE

Physical Education
Component 1: Fitness and Body Systems

Practice Paper
Time allowed: 1 hour 45 minutes

You are **allowed** to use a calculator.

Instructions to candidates
- Use **black** ink to write your answers.
- Write your name and other details in the spaces provided above.
- Answer **all** questions in the spaces provided.
- In calculations show clearly how you worked out your answers.

Information for candidates
- The marks available are given in brackets at the end of each question.
- There are 90 marks available for this paper.

Advice
- Carefully read each question before answering it.
- Try to answer every question.
- If you have time after finishing the paper, go back and check your answers.

Answer ALL the questions.

Write your answers in the spaces provided.

You must answer some questions with a cross in a box ☒. If you change your mind about an answer, put a line through the box ☒, then mark your new answer with a cross ☒.

1   (a)   Which one of the following bones is found in the lower leg?

☒   **A**   Clavicle

☒   **B**   Ulna

☒   **C**   Tibia

☒   **D**   Femur

[1]

(b)   Which one of the following muscles is responsible for flexion at the knee?

☒   **A**   Quadriceps

☒   **B**   Hamstrings

☒   **C**   Hip flexors

☒   **D**   Gluteus maximus

[1]

(c)   Which one of the following describes a third class lever system?

☒   **A**   The load is between the fulcrum and effort

☒   **B**   The fulcrum is between the effort and load

☒   **C**   The effort is at the end of the lever

☒   **D**   The effort is between the fulcrum and load

[1]

(d)   Identify the type of movement that would occur in the sagittal plane.

☒   **A**   Flexion

☒   **B**   Abduction

☒   **C**   Rotation

☒   **D**   Adduction

[1]

(e) Which one of the following components of fitness is measured by the Harvard step test?

☒ **A**   Muscular endurance

☒ **B**   Power

☒ **C**   Cardiovascular fitness

☒ **D**   Balance

[1]

(f) Which one of the following methods of training can be used to improve both aerobic and anaerobic fitness?

☒ **A**   Continuous training

☒ **B**   Resistance training

☒ **C**   Plyometric training

☒ **D**   Circuit training

[1]

(g) Which one of the following performance-enhancing drugs can be used to increase an athlete's red blood cell count?

☒ **A**   Erythropoietin (EPO)

☒ **B**   Narcotic analgesics

☒ **C**   Growth hormones

☒ **D**   Diuretics

[1]

Hanif is a 22-year-old basketball player. He has just taken the vertical jump test.

Table 1 shows ratings for the vertical jump test for adult athletes.

Gender	Excellent	Above Average	Average	Below Average	Poor
Male	>70 cm	56-70 cm	41-55 cm	31-40 cm	<31 cm
Female	>60 cm	46-60 cm	31-45 cm	21-30 cm	<21 cm

Table 1

(h) Which one of the following is the correct rating for Hanif, given that he scored 61 cm in the vertical jump test?

☒ **A**   Poor

☒ **B**   Average

☒ **C**   Above Average

☒ **D**   Excellent

[1]

[Total 8 marks]

2   Tendons are part of the musculo-skeletal system.

Explain the role of tendons in movement of the skeleton.

....

....

....

....

....

....

....

[Total 2 marks]

3   **Figure 1** shows an athlete preparing to jump during plyometric training.

Figure 1

Analyse, using **one** example, how **one** of the antagonistic muscle pairs in the body enables the athlete to jump.

....

....

....

....

....

....

....

[Total 3 marks]

58

4 Different muscle fibre types are suited to different activities.

(a) Identify the muscle fibre type that would be most suited to the long jump.

....

[1]

(b) Explain your answer.

....

....

....

[2]

[Total 3 marks]

5 Describe what it means for a lever to have a mechanical advantage.

....

....

....

[Total 2 marks]

6 Explain how the process of vascular shunting occurs during exercise.

....

....

....

....

....

....

[Total 3 marks]

7   Assess the positive and negative impact on performance of
    using anaerobic respiration during a swimming race.

    (i) Positive

    ....

    ....

    ....

    ....

    ....

    ....

    ....

                                                                                                            [3]

    (ii) Negative

    ....

    ....

    ....

    ....

    ....

    ....

    ....

                                                                                                            [3]
                                                                                               [Total 6 marks]

8 Explain how an increase in both breathing rate and heart rate provides the muscles with the oxygen they need during physical activity and sport.

....

....

....

....

....

....

....

[Total 4 marks]

9 **Figure 2** shows a diver standing on their toes in preparation for a dive.

Figure 2

(a) Classify the lever being used in **Figure 2**.

....

[1]

(b) Explain your answer.

....

....

....

[1]

[Total 2 marks]

10 Jack uses a heart rate monitor during a 50-minute training session with his running club. **Figure 3** shows his heart rate values during the session.

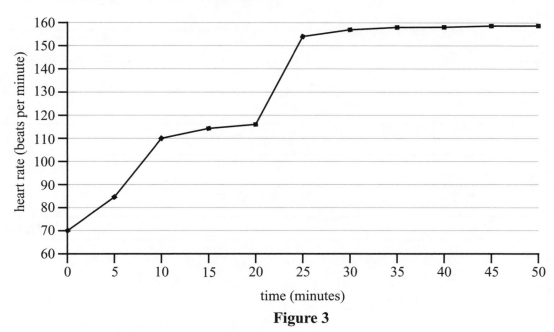

Figure 3

Using **Figure 3**, analyse Jack's heart rate at the following times to suggest what may have happened in his training session during those times. Justify your answers.

(i) Between 0 and 20 minutes.

....

....

....

[2]

(ii) Between 20 and 50 minutes.

....

....

....

[2]

[Total 4 marks]

62

11 Explain how the long-term effects of regular exercise on the heart would benefit an endurance athlete's performance.

....

....

....

....

....

....

....

[Total 3 marks]

12 **Figure 4** shows a tennis player using a third class lever system at the shoulder to swing the tennis racket and hit the ball.

Figure 4

Analyse how this third class lever system affects the tennis player's performance.

....

....

....

....

....

....

....

[Total 3 marks]

13 Explain how a high level of flexibility can improve a long jumper's performance.

....

....

....

....

....

....

....

[Total 3 marks]

14 The sit and reach test and the vertical jump test are two fitness tests.
Assess the relative importance of each of these fitness tests for a beach volleyball player.

(i) Sit and reach test

....

....

....

....

....

....

....

[3]

(ii) Vertical jump test

....

....

....

....

....

....

....

[3]

[Total 6 marks]

15 Hannah has been using the Illinois agility run test and the 30 m sprint test to monitor how her training is going. **Table 2** shows the results of her fitness tests.

Fitness Test	Week 1	Week 3	Week 5	Week 7	Week 9
Illinois agility run test	22 s	20.7 s	20.2 s	19.4 s	18.5 s
30 m sprint test	5.60 s	5.55 s	5.45 s	5.40 s	5.40 s

Table 2

(a) Describe how to carry out the Illinois agility run test.

....

....

....

....

[2]

(b) Analyse the data in **Table 2** to determine the trends for both fitness tests.

....

....

....

....

[2]

Hannah would like to improve her balance and her flexibility.

(c) Identify **one** fitness class she could attend to improve these two components of fitness.

....

[1]

[Total 5 marks]

16 Progressive overload is one of the principles of training.

(a) Define **progressive overload**.

....

....

[1]

(b) Give **one** example of using progressive overload in a javelin thrower's training.

....

....

....

[2]

[Total 3 marks]

---

17 Colin is 40 years old.

(a) Calculate his theoretical maximum heart rate.

....

[1]

(b) Calculate the upper and lower threshold's of his anaerobic target zone.

....

....

....

....

....

[4]

[Total 5 marks]

66

18 Explain **two** actions that a rugby player can take to help them avoid injury while playing their sport.

1 ....

....

....

....

2 ....

....

....

....

[Total 4 marks]

19 Identify whether anabolic steroids would give the most significant performance benefit to a 100 m sprinter or an endurance athlete. Explain your answer.

....

....

....

....

[Total 3 marks]

Component 1 Practice Paper

20 Evaluate the extent to which an increase in tidal volume would allow a midfielder in football to perform well during a match.

....
....
....
....
....
....
....
....
....
....
....
....
....
....
....
....
....
....
....
....
....
....
....
....
....
....
....
....

[Total 9 marks]

68

21 Evaluate the use of fartlek training and plyometric training to improve performance in netball.

....

....

....

....

....

....

....

....

....

....

....

....

....

....

....

....

....

....

....

....

....

....

....

....

....

[Total 9 marks]

TOTAL FOR PAPER = 90 MARKS

Candidate Surname		Candidate Forename(s)	

Centre Number	Candidate Number	Candidate Signature

GCSE

Physical Education
Component 2: Health and Performance

Practice Paper
Time allowed: 1 hour 15 minutes

You are **allowed** to use a calculator.

Instructions to candidates
- Use **black** ink to write your answers.
- Write your name and other details in the spaces provided above.
- Answer **all** questions in the spaces provided.

Information for candidates
- The marks available are given in brackets at the end of each question.
- There are 70 marks available for this paper.

Advice
- Carefully read each question before answering it.
- Try to answer every question.
- If you have time after finishing the paper, go back and check your answers.

Answer ALL the questions.

Write your answers in the spaces provided.

You must answer some questions with a cross in a box ☒. If you change your mind about an answer, put a line through the box ☒, then mark your new answer with a cross ☒.

1   (a) Which one of the following describes the technique of carbohydrate loading?

☒ **A**   Increasing carbohydrate intake after an endurance event
☒ **B**   Increasing carbohydrate intake before an endurance event
☒ **C**   Reducing carbohydrate intake after an endurance event
☒ **D**   Eating only carbohydrates in the days before an endurance event

[1]

(b) 'SMART' stands for the five principles of goal setting.
Which one of the following principles is represented by the 'A' in 'SMART'?

☒ **A**   Actual
☒ **B**   Accurate
☒ **C**   Achievable
☒ **D**   Accessible

[1]

(c) Which one of the following describes terminal feedback?

☒ **A**   Feedback that a performer gives to themselves
☒ **B**   Feedback that is received during a performance
☒ **C**   Feedback that is received after a performance
☒ **D**   Feedback that a coach gives to a performer

[1]

Alison takes part in very little physical activity because her nearest sports centre is five miles away and she doesn't own a car. Public transport links to the sports centre are also very poor.

(d) Which one of the following types of influence has affected
Alison's participation in physical activity?

☒ **A**   Disability
☒ **B**   Age
☒ **C**   Gender
☒ **D**   Socio-economic

[1]

(e) Which one of the following is an example of gamesmanship?

☒ **A** Time-wasting in football

☒ **B** Using performance-enhancing drugs

☒ **C** Deliberately tripping an opponent in football

☒ **D** Blood doping

[1]

(f) **Figure 1** shows data on the frequency of alcohol consumption in the years 2005 to 2014.

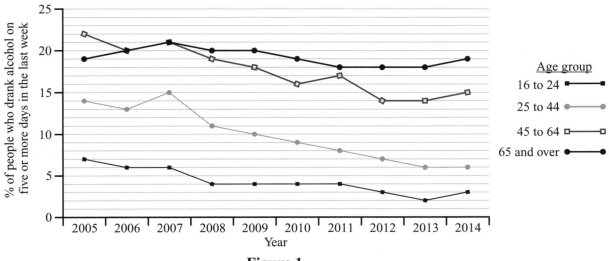

Figure 1

Using **Figure 1**, identify the age group that saw the largest **decrease** in the percentage who drank alcohol on five or more days, between 2005 and 2014.

☒ **A** 16 to 24

☒ **B** 25 to 44

☒ **C** 45 to 64

☒ **D** 65 and over

[1]

[Total 6 marks]

2 Exercise can improve physical, emotional and social health and well-being.

(a) Give **one** example of a physical benefit of exercise.

....

....

[1]

(b) Explain **one** way that exercise can improve emotional health.

....

....

....

[2]

(c) Exercise can help you to learn the skills of teamwork and cooperation.
State whether this is a physical, emotional or social benefit of exercise.

....

[1]

[Total 4 marks]

3 Walter is a member of a local swimming club. He has just started smoking.

Explain **two** ways that smoking may affect performance in swimming.

1 ....

....

....

....

2 ....

....

....

....

[Total 4 marks]

4   Water is one of the nutrients required for a balanced diet.

(a) Complete the following statements about the effects of dehydration.

Dehydration can cause the blood to become .... It can also cause your

body temperature to ....

[2]

(b) Give **one** way that exercise causes the body to lose water.

....

....

[1]

[Total 3 marks]

5   The optimum weights of a rugby player and a hockey player are different.

(a) State which sport will have the higher optimum weight.

....

[1]

(b) Explain why two rugby players in the same team might have different optimum weights.

....

....

....

[2]

(c) Explain how a hockey player could manipulate their energy
balance to increase how much they weigh.

....

....

....

[2]

[Total 5 marks]

74

6 Variable and fixed practice can be used to improve performance in sport.

Assess the relative importance of these practice types for improving performance in tennis.

(i) Variable practice

....

....

....

....

[3]

(ii) Fixed practice

....

....

....

....

[3]

[Total 6 marks]

7 Amanda sets herself a goal to complete an 80-mile bike ride in four months' time.

Analyse how the application of one of the principles of
SMART in Amanda's goal will help her to achieve her goal.

....

....

....

....

....

....

[Total 3 marks]

8 **Figures 2a and 2b** show data on participation rates
in swimming and football between 07/08 and 14/15.

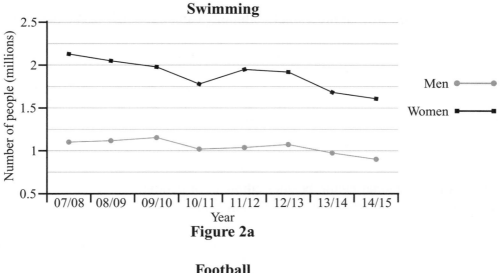

Figure 2a

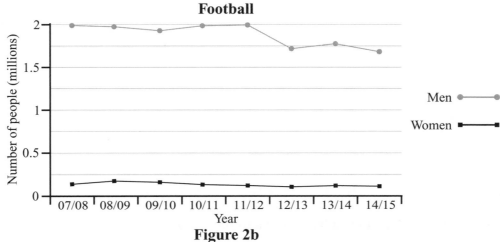

Figure 2b

(a) Analyse **Figure 2a** to determine the trend in participation in swimming between 2007 and 2015.

....

[1]

(b) Analyse **Figures 2a** and **2b** to determine the differences in participation levels between men and
women in swimming and football. Give **one** possible reason for these differences in each sport.

Swimming

....

....

....

[2]

Football

....

....

....

[2]

[Total 5 marks]

9   Studies by Sport England have shown that people from some ethnic groups
    are more likely to participate in physical activity than others.

    (a) Explain **one** reason why an individual's ethnicity can affect their participation in sport.

    ....

    ....

    ....

    ....
                                                                                                                    [2]

    (b) Give **one** other personal factor, besides ethnicity or gender,
        that can affect an individual's participation in sport.

    ....
                                                                                                                    [1]
                                                                                                    [Total 3 marks]

10 Sponsorship, sport and the media have grown to rely on one another.

    (a) Give **one** example of an inappropriate sponsor for an under-16s badminton tournament.

    ....
                                                                                                                    [1]

    (b) Explain your answer.

    ....

    ....

    ....
                                                                                                                    [2]
                                                                                                    [Total 3 marks]

11 Assess the positive and negative impact of increased media interest in a sport.

(i) Positive impact

....

....

....

....

[3]

(ii) Negative impact

....

....

....

....

[3]

[Total 6 marks]

12 Some sportspeople display gamesmanship while competing.

(a) Define **gamesmanship**.

....

....

[1]

(b) Assess the impact of elite performers demonstrating
gamesmanship in high profile sports, such as cricket.

....

....

....

....

....

....

[3]

[Total 4 marks]

13 Evaluate whether a long-distance cyclist should use a combination of carbohydrate loading and timing of protein intake to improve race performance.

....

....

....

....

....

....

....

....

....

....

....

....

....

....

....

....

....

....

....

....

....

....

....

....

....

....

....

[Total 9 marks]

14 Evaluate the use of visual and mechanical guidance
when coaching a group of beginners in trampolining.

....

....

....

....

....

....

....

....

....

....

....

....

....

....

....

....

....

....

....

....

....

....

....

....

....

....

[Total 9 marks]

TOTAL FOR PAPER = 70 MARKS

Component 2 Practice Paper

A note about marks and grades
The answers and mark schemes given here should be used mainly for guidance, as there may be many different correct answers to each question — don't panic if your answers are a bit different. The grade stamps are a rough guide to the level of difficulty of each question, and should not be used to predict the grade you'll get in the real exams.

Section One — Anatomy and Physiology

Pages 3-5: The Skeletal System

1 **C** Rib *[1 mark]*

2 **D** Hip *[1 mark]*

3 **B** Dorsi-flexion *[1 mark]*

4 Flexion and extension *[1 mark]*

5 E.g. Preparing to swing a hockey stick *[1 mark]*
You would get the mark for any example that involves moving the arm away from an imaginary centre line on the body.

6 E.g. During a game of hockey, if a player were to be hit on the head by the ball *[1 mark]*, the cranium would protect the brain from a serious injury *[1 mark]*.

7 E.g. Ligaments hold bones together at joints *[1 mark]*. They maintain the stability of the skeleton *[1 mark]*, which helps to prevent injury during joint movements *[1 mark]*.

8 E.g. The attachment of muscles to bones enables movement of the skeleton *[1 mark]*. This allows a performer to perform the joint movements necessary to participate in physical activity *[1 mark]*.

9 E.g. The hinge joint at the knee allows flexion and extension *[1 mark]*, so the footballer can bend and then straighten her leg *[1 mark]* and therefore generate the power needed to kick the ball *[1 mark]*.

10 E.g. The hip moves from flexion at the top of the pedal stroke *[1 mark]* to extension at the bottom *[1 mark]*.

Pages 6-7: The Muscular System

1 (a) Extension at the knee *[1 mark]*

(b) E.g. Jumping to score a slam dunk in basketball *[1 mark]*.
You will get the mark for part (b) for any sporting example that involves straightening the leg at the knee.

2 E.g. In position A, the biceps are contracting and the triceps are relaxing *[1 mark]* to flex the elbows *[1 mark]*. In position B, the triceps are contracting and biceps are relaxing *[1 mark]* to extend the elbows *[1 mark]*.

3 *This mark scheme gives examples of some points you might have made in your answer, and how many marks you would get for making those points. You can still get full marks if you haven't written every individual point below, as long as the points you have made are detailed enough.*

You will get up to three marks for showing knowledge and understanding of type I and type IIA muscle fibres, for example:

• Type I muscle fibres are slow twitch muscle fibres suited to low intensity aerobic activity.
• Type IIA muscle fibres are fast twitch muscle fibres suited to high intensity anaerobic activity.
• Type IIA muscle fibres can be trained to increase their resistance to fatigue.

You will get up to six marks if you also include examples of when each muscle fibre type will be used during a marathon, for example:

• Type I muscle fibres can be used for a long time, so would be used throughout the race to maintain a steady running pace.
• Type IIA muscle fibres would be used during a marathon when overtaking other runners, during a sprint finish, or when running on hilly terrain.
• Type IIA muscle fibres fatigue more quickly than type I, so would only be used for short bursts during the marathon, but not for the entire race.

You will get up to nine marks if you also evaluate the importance of type I and type IIA muscle fibre types to performance in a marathon, for example:

• Type I muscle fibres are the most useful for a marathon runner, as they allow them to run at a steady pace for the duration of the race.
• Type IIA fibres are also important for a marathon runner — if they are trained to resist fatigue, a runner would be able to use them for longer in order to compete against other runners, for example, when increasing their speed to overtake other runners.
• In conclusion, both fibre types are important for a marathon runner as type I allow endurance and type IIA allow speed and power.
[9 marks available in total]

Pages 8-9: The Cardiovascular System

1 **D** Pulmonary artery *[1 mark]*

2 **A** Vena cava *[1 mark]*

3 Any **two** from: e.g.
• Transfer oxygen into the body's tissues.
• Transfer glucose into the body's tissues.
• Transfer nutrients into the body's tissues.
• Remove carbon dioxide from the body's tissues.
• Remove waste products from the body's tissues.
• Remove lactic acid from the body's tissues.
[2 marks available in total]

4 E.g. The cardiovascular system releases heat by shunting blood closer to the skin's surface *[1 mark]*. This allows a performer to exercise for long periods without overheating *[1 mark]*.

5 E.g. Arteries have thick, muscular walls *[1 mark]*, which allows them to carry blood flowing at high pressure *[1 mark]*.

6 (a) E.g. Arm muscles *[1 mark]* and leg muscles *[1 mark]*.

(b) E.g. The muscles in the arms and legs would be working while swimming *[1 mark]*, so they would need more oxygenated blood *[1 mark]* in order to release the extra energy needed for swimming movements *[1 mark]*.
You could also have said that the muscles in the arms and legs would release more waste products, such as carbon dioxide or lactic acid, so they would need extra blood to remove them.

7 E.g. Red blood cells carry oxygen *[1 mark]*, so a high number of red blood cells would lead to more oxygen being delivered to the muscles during exercise *[1 mark]*. This is very important for an endurance athlete, as it would allow them to work aerobically for long periods *[1 mark]*.

Pages 10-11: The Respiratory System

1 (a) Tidal volume is the volume of air breathed in or out in one breath *[1 mark]*. Vital capacity is the largest volume of air that can be breathed in after breathing out the most air possible *[1 mark]*.

   (b) Tidal volume increases during exercise *[1 mark]*.

2 Air flows through the mouth or nose into the **trachea**, then into the **bronchi**. These then split into progressively smaller tubes called **bronchioles**, which the air flows through to reach the alveoli.
[3 marks available in total — 1 mark for each correct word]

3 E.g. During inhalation, the diaphragm contracts to expand the chest cavity and draw air into the lungs *[1 mark]*. During exhalation, it relaxes into its normal shape, shrinking the chest cavity and forcing air back out of the lungs *[1 mark]*.

4 E.g. Exhaled air has less oxygen than inhaled air *[1 mark]* because some of the oxygen will have been used by the body to release energy through aerobic respiration *[1 mark]*. Exhaled air also contains more carbon dioxide than inhaled air *[1 mark]*, as this is produced as a by-product of aerobic respiration and needs to be breathed out *[1 mark]*.

5 E.g. The thin walls of alveoli allow gases to pass through them easily *[1 mark]*. This makes it easier for oxygen to pass from the alveoli into the blood in the capillaries surrounding them *[1 mark]* and for carbon dioxide to pass from the blood in the capillaries into the alveoli *[1 mark]*.

6 E.g. A high vital capacity would be very beneficial to a triathlete because it would provide a high maximum tidal volume during exercise *[1 mark]*. This would mean a large volume of oxygen could be taken into their lungs, then transferred to their blood and delivered to their muscles *[1 mark]*. This would allow them to release the energy needed throughout the long duration of the event *[1 mark]*.

Page 12: Aerobic and Anaerobic Exercise

1 **B** Low intensity aerobic *[1 mark]*

2 *This mark scheme gives examples of some points you might have made in your answer, and how many marks you would get for making those points. You can still get full marks if you haven't written every individual point below, as long as the points you have made are detailed enough.*

You will get up to three marks for showing knowledge of aerobic and anaerobic respiration, for example:
- Aerobic respiration uses glucose and oxygen to release energy.
- Aerobic respiration is needed for activities that require endurance.
- Anaerobic respiration uses glucose to release energy, but doesn't use oxygen.

You will get up to six marks if you also include examples of when aerobic and anaerobic respiration would be needed during a 50-mile cycling race, for example:

- Cycling for 50 miles would take several hours, so aerobic respiration would be needed for the majority of the race.
- Anaerobic respiration would be needed for high-intensity parts of the race, for example, when cycling on a steep gradient.
- Anaerobic respiration would be used for short bursts of speed on the bike.

You will get up to nine marks if you evaluate the importance of aerobic and anaerobic respiration for performance in a 50-mile cycling race, for example:

- A cyclist in a 50-mile race would want to mainly use aerobic respiration to ensure they can maintain a good performance throughout the race.
- The cyclist may want to avoid cycling at speeds where anaerobic respiration is needed too often, as this would cause muscle fatigue, leading to a drop in performance.
- In conclusion, both types of respiration are important to achieve good overall performance in a 50-mile cycling race, as the performer must balance endurance with speed.
[9 marks available in total]

Pages 13-14: Short-Term Effects of Exercise

1 E.g. Oxygen debt occurs as a result of anaerobic activity, which leads to the production of lactic acid and causes muscle fatigue *[1 mark]*. Oxygen debt is the amount of oxygen that must be breathed in to remove the lactic acid and recover from this activity *[1 mark]*.

2 E.g. During physical activity, there is an increased demand for oxygen in the muscles *[1 mark]* due to the need to release more energy *[1 mark]*. Therefore, heart rate increases in order to deliver more oxygenated blood to the muscles *[1 mark]*.

3 (a) During the run: 23.62 l/min *[1 mark]*
       After the run: 10.34 l/min *[1 mark]*

   (b) The highest value is during the run because cardiac output increases to meet the increased demand for oxygen in the muscles *[1 mark]*. The middle value is after the run because cardiac output decreases after exercise has stopped, but stays above resting cardiac output to help with recovery *[1 mark]*.

4 E.g. The performer's heart rate was much higher throughout workout A *[1 mark]*, which suggests that they exercised at a higher intensity than in workout B *[1 mark]*.

5 E.g. A 100 m sprint is an anaerobic event *[1 mark]*, so increased tidal volume would not improve performance because the additional oxygen taken into the lungs would not be used during the sprint *[1 mark]*. However, it is important as it would help improve the rate of recovery after the sprint by removing lactic acid produced by anaerobic respiration *[1 mark]*.

Page 15: Long-Term Effects of Exercise

1 Any **two** from: e.g.
- Increased resting stroke volume
- Increased maximum cardiac output
- Decreased resting heart rate
- Increased lung capacity
- Increased strength of diaphragm
- Increased strength of external intercostal muscles
- Increase in number of alveoli in lungs
- Increased vital capacity

82

- Decreased blood pressure
- Increase in number of capillaries in muscles
- Increase in number of red blood cells
- Increased cardiovascular fitness
[2 marks available in total]

2   E.g. An increase in muscle girth would lead to an increase in strength *[1 mark]*, which would benefit, for example, a rugby player during a tackle *[1 mark]* as it would help them to pull an opponent to the ground *[1 mark]*.

3   E.g. Running is an aerobic activity which causes the heart to work harder *[1 mark]*, which leads to muscle hypertrophy of the heart in the long term *[1 mark]*. This increases resting stroke volume *[1 mark]* and therefore decreases resting heart rate, as the heart can deliver the same amount of blood to the rest of the body with fewer beats *[1 mark]*.

Section Two — Movement Analysis

Page 16 — Lever Systems

1   The square is used to represent the **load** of the lever system. The arrow represents the **effort** and the triangle represents the **fulcrum**.
[3 marks available in total — 1 mark for each correct word]

2   The load is the weight of the lower leg below the knee *[1 mark]*, the fulcrum is the knee joint *[1 mark]* and the effort is the force of the quadriceps *[1 mark]*.

3   (a) Second class *[1 mark]*
    (b) Second class levers have a mechanical advantage, so can move large loads *[1 mark]* with a small effort from the muscles *[1 mark]*. This allows the performer to easily raise their entire body weight onto their toes *[1 mark]*.

Page 17 — Planes and Axes of Movement

1   **D** Sagittal *[1 mark]*
2   **D** Vertical *[1 mark]*
3   (i) Frontal plane *[1 mark]* and sagittal axis *[1 mark]*
    (ii) Sagittal plane *[1 mark]* and frontal axis *[1 mark]*
    (iii) Transverse plane *[1 mark]* and vertical axis *[1 mark]*

Section Three — Physical Training

Page 18: Health and Fitness

1   **D** Having a high level of fitness means you can meet the demands of your environment *[1 mark]*

2   (a) Health is a state of complete physical, emotional and social well-being *[1 mark]*.
    (b) E.g. Christine could have a high level of physical fitness, but still be unhappy or suffering from high stress levels *[1 mark]*. To be classified as healthy, Christine would need to have a good state of emotional and social well-being, as well as being physically fit and healthy *[1 mark]*.

3   E.g. Exercise improves individual components of fitness and overall fitness, which leads to an improvement in performance *[1 mark]*. Exercise also improves physical health, which helps reduce the risk of illness and injury. Being in good health allows a sportsperson to perform better *[1 mark]* and to train more, which also leads to performance

gains *[1 mark]*. Exercise can also improve emotional and social health, which will lead to better performances as the sportsperson will feel happier and more confident in their abilities *[1 mark]*.

Pages 19-22: Components of Fitness

1   **B** At the start of the race, when the starter pistol is fired *[1 mark]*

2   **C** Agility *[1 mark]*

3   Body composition is the percentage of **body weight** made up by **fat**, muscle and bone.
[2 marks available in total — 1 mark for each correct word or phrase]

4   (a) Balance is the ability to keep the body's centre of mass over a base of support *[1 mark]*.
    (b) E.g. A gymnast needs good balance to keep themselves stable on the beam *[1 mark]*.

5   Muscular endurance *[1 mark]*

6   E.g. Coordination is the ability to use two or more parts of the body together, efficiently and accurately *[1 mark]*. A tennis player needs good hand-eye coordination and to coordinate their arm and leg movements to move to the ball and hit a well-timed shot *[1 mark]*.

7   (a) E.g. Power *[1 mark]* and balance *[1 mark]*.
    (b) E.g. Throwing the shot with more power will mean that Ben achieves a greater height with his throw, so it will travel further *[1 mark]*.
    E.g. The action in shot-put involves rotating to generate power. Balance will help Ben to control this rotation, so his throwing action will be smooth and coordinated *[1 mark]*.
    There are other answers you could give to this question as several components of fitness are involved in the shot-put. Just make sure your justification clearly shows how that component of fitness improves performance.

8   E.g. The main action affecting a golfer's performance is their swing *[1 mark]*. This can be improved by increased flexibility in the shoulders *[1 mark]*, which would allow the golfer to draw the club further back and to have a smooth swing through the whole range of motion at the shoulder *[1 mark]*.

9   (a) E.g. Agility is the ability to change body position or direction quickly and with control *[1 mark]*.
    (b) E.g. Agility is more important for Jamie than Roberta *[1 mark]* as Jamie needs to change direction to dodge round opponents *[1 mark]*, whereas Roberta does not need to change direction because the 100 m takes place on a straight course *[1 mark]*.

10 (i) E.g. Good cardiovascular fitness means you can exercise the whole body for a long time *[1 mark]*. A long jumper only has to run for a short amount of time *[1 mark]*, so cardiovascular fitness is not the most important component of fitness for their performance *[1 mark]*.
   (ii) E.g. Power is the ability to do strength actions with speed *[1 mark]*. During a long jump, both the sprint up to the board and the take-off from the board require lots of power *[1 mark]*, so power is one of the most important components of fitness for a long jumper *[1 mark]*.

Answers

11 (a) Lizzy *[1 mark]*

(b) Flexibility is important in football, for example when a player lunges to try and tackle someone *[1 mark]*. However, many actions in gymnastics, e.g. the splits, require a lot of flexibility, therefore Lizzy will require more flexibility to perform well *[1 mark]*.

12 *This mark scheme gives examples of some points you might have made in your answer, and how many marks you'd get for making those points. You can still get full marks if you haven't written every individual point below, as long as the points you've made are detailed enough.*

You will get up to three marks for showing knowledge and understanding of what cardiovascular fitness and strength are, for example:

- Good cardiovascular fitness means the heart and lungs can supply the muscles with oxygen so the whole body can be exercised for a long time.
- Strength is the amount of force a group of muscles can exert against a resistance.
- Good cardiovascular fitness allows a performer to recover from strenuous exercise more quickly.

You will get up to six marks if you also include examples of how these components of fitness would affect the weightlifter's performance, for example:

- A high level of cardiovascular fitness means the weightlifter could train for longer as they would recover quicker between sets.
- As weightlifting is a short duration, anaerobic event, cardiovascular fitness would not directly help the weightlifter to compete.
- A high level of strength is required for a weightlifter to be able to lift the heavy weights.

You will get up to nine marks if you also weigh up which component of fitness is more important, for example:

- A good level of cardiovascular fitness is important, as it will allow the weightlifter to train effectively and recover quickly following strenuous exercise.
- However, while cardiovascular fitness will help the weightlifter to train more effectively, it cannot directly improve the weightlifter's performance.
- In conclusion, strength is far more important than cardiovascular fitness for the weightlifter, as it allows a large weight to be lifted and is therefore critical to their performance in a competition.
[9 marks available in total]

Pages 23-24: Fitness Testing

1 **A** Power *[1 mark]*

2 **B** Sit and reach test *[1 mark]*

3 E.g. The person taking the test has one minute to do as many sit-ups as possible. The number of sit-ups they do is recorded, and the higher this number is, the better the muscular endurance of their abdominal muscles.
[2 marks available in total — 1 mark for a correct description and 1 mark for correctly saying what the result shows]

4 Grip dynamometer test *[1 mark]*

5 (a) E.g. Eric could compare his fitness test score to national averages to understand where he ranked *[1 mark]*. Eric could use fitness testing to monitor his progress,

so he would know whether his training was effective *[1 mark]*.

(b) E.g. The Cooper 12-minute run test measures cardiovascular fitness (aerobic endurance) *[1 mark]*, whereas the 30 m sprint test measures maximum sprint speed over a short distance *[1 mark]*. The triathlon is an endurance event that requires a high level of cardiovascular fitness, so the Cooper 12-minute test is more suitable for Eric *[1 mark]*.

(c) Eric's training is not improving his cardiovascular fitness *[1 mark]*.

6 (i) E.g. The sit and reach test measures the flexibility of the back and lower hamstrings *[1 mark]*. Footballers require flexible legs to make their running and their kicking actions smooth and efficient *[1 mark]*. Therefore, the sit and reach test is a suitable test for a footballer. *[1 mark]*.

(ii) E.g. The Illinois agility run test measures agility *[1 mark]*. The ability to quickly change direction and weave around opponents is one of the most important skills for a footballer *[1 mark]*, therefore this is a more important fitness test than the sit and reach test for a footballer *[1 mark]*.

Page 25: Fitness Testing — Data Questions

1 **A** Good *[1 mark]*

2 E.g. 52 kg *[1 mark]*
You could give any number in the range 51-56 kg for a mark here.

3 (a) Amir's score in the sit and reach test is increasing each week, so he is reaching a little further each week *[1 mark]*. Amir's score has stayed almost constant each week in the one minute sit-up test, so the number of sit-ups he can do is neither increasing nor decreasing *[1 mark]*.

(b) Amir's flexibility is improving *[1 mark]*.

Pages 26-27: Principles of Training

1 Any **three** from: e.g.
- You can increase the frequency that you train.
- You can increase the intensity of training.
- You can increase the amount of time each training session lasts.
- You can vary the type of training that you do.
[3 marks available in total]

2 (a) E.g. Progressive overload means gradually increasing the amount of work you do in training to improve fitness *[1 mark]*. Lucy could do this by gradually increasing the distance she runs each week *[1 mark]*.

(b) (i) Specificity means matching training to the activity and components of fitness you want to improve *[1 mark]*.

(ii) E.g. Lucy could apply specificity to her training by making sure that most of her training involves running long distances without taking breaks *[1 mark]*.

3 (a) Ele's cardiovascular fitness may begin to decrease *[1 mark]* because any fitness gains made during training will gradually reverse when she stops training *[1 mark]*.

(b) Ele should leave a longer period between training sessions *[1 mark]* in order to give her body enough time to recover and make adaptations *[1 mark]*.

4 *This mark scheme gives examples of some points you might have made in your answer, and how many marks you'd get for making those points. You can still get full marks if you haven't written every individual point below, as long as the points you've made are detailed enough.*

You will get up to three marks for showing knowledge and understanding of the principles of training, for example:

• The principle of individual needs means tailoring training to the personal requirements of a performer.
• Specificity means that the training needs to match what the performer is actually training for.
• The principle of progressive overload means that training should gradually become more difficult to increase fitness, while allowing the body time to adapt.

You will get up to six marks if you also include examples of how Jeffrey could use the principles of training for rock climbing, for example:

• Individual needs means that Jeffrey's level of training will be suitable for his age and his level of fitness and skill, so he will not attempt to climb anything he is not ready for.
• Specificity means that Jeffrey will do lots of resistance exercises that involve lifting his own body weight — e.g. pull-ups to improve upper body strength, using resistance hand grips to improve finger strength and climbing on an indoor climbing wall.
• Jeffrey will gradually increase the number of reps on pull-ups / number of reps on hand grips / difficulty of indoor climbs to progressively overload his muscles and let them increase in strength without overdoing it and causing injury.

You will get up to nine marks if you also evaluate the use of the three principles to prevent injury in Jeffrey's training, for example:

• Jeffrey could suffer serious injuries if he attempts to climb something that is too difficult for him, so individual needs and progressive overload are very important principles for him, especially at the start of his training.
• Specificity is perhaps the least important of these principles of training in terms of helping Jeffrey avoid injury, as its main purpose is to improve his skill.
• In conclusion, Jeffrey should makes sure he applies all three principles to his training, although individual needs and progressive overload will be the most effective in helping him to avoid injury.
[9 marks available in total]

Page 28: Training Target Zones

1 Fatima should spend more time training anaerobically *[1 mark]* as weightlifting requires short bursts of maximal effort, so is an anaerobic activity *[1 mark]*.

2 (a) $220 - 25 = 195$ *[1 mark]*.
      195×0.6 *[1 mark]* $= 117$ bpm *[1 mark]*
      You do 195×0.6 because the lower aerobic threshold is 60% of maximum heart rate.

   (b) Week 2, week 3, week 4 and week 5.
      [2 marks for all four correct weeks, or 1 mark for finding the upper threshold of Leonardo's aerobic target zone]

Pages 29-31: Training Methods

1 **C** A type of continuous training that involves changes in intensity *[1 mark]*

2 Any **three** from the following: e.g.
   • The distance covered in training can be increased.
   • The time spent training can be increased.
   • The speed or pace of training can be increased.
   • The frequency of the training can be increased.
   [3 marks available in total]

3 Resistance training can be used to improve strength, power and **muscular endurance**. To improve strength, a **high** weight is used, with a **low** number of reps.
   [3 marks available in total — 1 mark for each correct word or phrase]
   You would still get marks for using different words that mean the same thing as 'high' and 'low' here, e.g. if you wrote 'large' and 'small' instead.

4 E.g. Interval training *[1 mark]*. As basketball involves a mixture of sprinting and jogging, with quick changes in pace, interval training is well suited *[1 mark]*.
   E.g. Plyometric training *[1 mark]*. Being able to jump high is critical in basketball, and plyometric training can help improve jump height by making a player's legs more powerful *[1 mark]*.
   There are different types of training you could mention here, as long as you can justify your choice you'll get both marks.

5
Training method	Component of fitness improved	Long-term training adaptation to body systems
E.g. **Resistance** or **Weight**	Strength	E.g. **Muscular Hypertrophy**
Continuous	E.g. **Cardiovascular Fitness**	E.g. **Increased number of red blood cells.**

[4 marks available in total — 1 mark for each correct word or phrase]

6 (a) E.g. Circuit training can be tailored to improve lots of different components of fitness in one session *[1 mark]*. E.g. Circuit training requires a lot of equipment and space *[1 mark]*.

   (b) (i) E.g. Skipping *[1 mark]*

      (ii) E.g. Squats *[1 mark]*

   (c) N'Golo could attend a spinning class *[1 mark]* as this is a high intensity cardiovascular workout involving cycling, so mainly focuses on the leg muscles *[1 mark]*.
      Any fitness class that improves cardiovascular fitness and leg strength is correct here — so you could have also said aerobics or BODYPUMP™.

7 E.g. Interval training *[1 mark]* because there are alternating periods of higher- and lower-intensity exercise shown on the graph *[1 mark]*.
   You could have also interpreted the graph as showing fartlek training or circuit training, as both also involve alternating periods of different intensity exercise.

8 *This mark scheme gives examples of some points you might have made in your answer, and how many marks you'd get for making those points. You can still get full marks if you haven't written every individual point below, as long as the points you've made are detailed enough.*

You will get up to three marks for showing knowledge of interval training and continuous training, for example:

- Interval training involves alternating periods of high- and low-intensity exercise.
- Continuous training involves training at a constant rate without any rests.
- Interval training can improve both aerobic and anaerobic fitness.

You will get up to six marks if you also include examples of how these methods of training can impact on the performance of a basketball player, for example:

- Basketball often requires sudden spurts of fast movement to beat an opponent to the ball. Interval training can help prepare the player for this by combining slower jogs with quicker sprints within one training session.
- Continuous training improves cardiovascular fitness, which will help the basketball player to use their muscles continuously throughout a game.
- Continuous training does not improve anaerobic fitness, so does not help prepare the basketball player for when they may need to sprint.

You will get up to nine marks if you also make judgements about the suitability of these training methods for a basketball player, for example:

- Interval training is better suited to the conditions of a basketball game, with its constantly changing pace. Therefore interval training is a crucial part of a basketball player's training.
- Continuous training is an important part of a basketball player's training as it improves cardiovascular fitness and helps to prepare them for constantly moving throughout the game.
- In conclusion, both types of training can be used effectively by a basketball player, however it would be sensible for a basketball player to also use weight training and plyometric training to develop the strength and power they need.

[9 marks available in total]

Page 32: Preventing Injuries

1 E.g. A PARQ is a questionnaire made up of yes or no questions designed to check it is safe for you to do a training programme *[1 mark]*. It is carried out before you start a training programme *[1 mark]*.

2 E.g. Light exercise to increase heart rate *[1 mark]*. Stretching the muscles that will be used in the activity *[1 mark]*. Practising the actions that will be used in the game *[1 mark]*.

3 (a) E.g. She can ensure students are wearing the correct protective clothing, like shin pads and gum shields *[1 mark]*. She can also inspect the pitch before they play to make sure that it's in good condition *[1 mark]* and she can referee the match *[1 mark]*.
   There are plenty of other examples you could give here about checking equipment and facilities, playing by the rules, using the correct clothing and equipment, and structuring training correctly.

   (b) E.g. Refereeing the game ensures that rules are followed *[1 mark]*. This reduces the chance of injury because it discourages players from committing fouls or carrying out dangerous actions that could injure other players *[1 mark]*. Inspecting the pitch makes sure that there aren't any tripping, slipping or other hazards *[1 mark]*. This reduces the risk of injury as it makes players less

likely to fall, or be cut by litter on the pitch, while playing *[1 mark]*.

Pages 33-34: Injuries and Treatment

1 **A** Stress fracture *[1 mark]*

2

Type of Injury	Damaged Tissue
Sprain	**Ligaments**
Strain	**Muscle** or **Tendon**
Golfer's Elbow	**Tendon**

[3 marks available in total — one for each correct word]

3

Type of fracture	Performer
Stress	**A 45-year-old marathon runner**
Compound	**B 22-year-old rugby player**

[2 marks available in total — 1 mark for each performer]

4 Riyad is more likely to get a concussion *[1 mark]*. This is because football involves contact with other players and there is a risk of high speed collisions with other players or the ball *[1 mark]*, whereas there is no contact in long distance running, so the only risk of concussion comes from tripping and falling while running *[1 mark]*.

5 (a) Rest *[1 mark]*
   Compression *[1 mark]*

   (b) E.g. Applying ice makes the blood vessels around the injury contract *[1 mark]*. This reduces blood flow to the injured area, so there is less internal bleeding and swelling *[1 mark]*.

6 E.g. The tackling player could get a cut *[1 mark]* if they come into contact with the other player's studded boots *[1 mark]*.
   E.g. The tackling player could sprain the ligaments in their arms or shoulders *[1 mark]* as the impact of the tackle could twist or stretch the ligaments at the shoulder or the elbow *[1 mark]*.

Page 35: Performance-Enhancing Drugs

1 **D** Beta Blockers lower the heart rate and have a calming, relaxing effect *[1 mark]*

2 E.g. Stimulants increase mental and physical awareness *[1 mark]*. Stimulants can lead to high blood pressure, which increases the risk of strokes *[1 mark]*.

3 E.g. A shot-putter will have greater performance gains from anabolic steroids *[1 mark]* because throwing the shot requires a large amount of strength and power, so performers need a large muscle mass *[1 mark]*.

4 (a) E.g. Strokes *[1 mark]* and heart attacks *[1 mark]*.

   (b) E.g. EPO causes the body to produce more red blood cells *[1 mark]*. This means that the body can transport more oxygen to the working muscles *[1 mark]* which would help an endurance athlete to work aerobically for longer *[1 mark]*.

Section Four — Health, Fitness and Well-being

Pages 36-37: Health, Fitness and Well-being

1 **D** Regular exercise can help to increase self-esteem *[1 mark]*

2 Exercise increases the level of endorphins and **serotonin** in your brain, which may make you feel happier and help to reduce the risk of depression.
[1 mark for the correct word]

3 (a) E.g. Exercise could help take Khalid's mind off the things he is worried about *[1 mark]* which could help to reduce his stress levels *[1 mark]*.

(b) E.g. It could give him an opportunity to meet new people and make new friends *[1 mark]*.
E.g. If he joins a team he will have the opportunity to practise teamwork and cooperation with others *[1 mark]*.

4 Osteoporosis is a disease that causes **bones** to become weak and fragile. Doing regular **weight-bearing** exercise can help to prevent osteoporosis.
*[2 marks available in total —
1 mark for each correct word or phrase]*

5 E.g. Exercise can create a feeling of having achieved something, for example, if a goal is achieved *[1 mark]*. This would lead to an increase in self-esteem as a performer would have a higher opinion of themselves and feel more confident *[1 mark]*.

6 (a) E.g. Exercise reduces the risk of coronary heart disease *[1 mark]*, for example, by removing cholesterol from arteries *[1 mark]* and therefore helping to reduce blood pressure *[1 mark]*.

(b) E.g. If you exercise too much without leaving enough time to recover between workouts, it can lead to overtraining *[1 mark]*. This can lead to weakness and tiredness, therefore increasing the likelihood of injury *[1 mark]*.

Page 38: Lifestyle Choices

1 **A** It raises heart rate and blood pressure *[1 mark]*

2 E.g. Alcohol would negatively affect the performance of a 100 m sprinter as it would slow their reaction time *[1 mark]* so they would not react quickly enough to the starter pistol, increasing the time it takes them to finish a race *[1 mark]*.
You could say that alcohol affects coordination or judgement — as long as you explain what effect that would have on performance in a physical activity or sport.

3 E.g. Lack of sleep will negatively affect a gymnast's performance because it can reduce coordination and concentration *[1 mark]*. This would affect a gymnast's ability to move their limbs in a controlled way or focus on their routine *[1 mark]*. This could mean that they would struggle to carry out complex gymnastics moves skilfully, such as a dismount from the uneven bars *[1 mark]*.

Page 39: Sedentary Lifestyle

1 (a) E.g. Being overweight means the cardiovascular system has to work harder to supply oxygen to the whole body, so cardiovascular fitness is reduced *[1 mark]*.

(b) E.g. If a footballer is overweight and has low cardiovascular fitness as a result, this would make them unable to exercise for long periods *[1 mark]*. This would negatively affect their performance, as they would become tired during a match and be unable to keep up with other players in the game or run with the ball *[1 mark]*.
There are loads of sports you could mention here, as long as you can give an example of how being overweight could affect performance, you'll get two marks.

2 (a) E.g. A sedentary lifestyle is a lifestyle that involves little or no physical activity *[1 mark]*.

(b) E.g. Joint damage *[1 mark]*
E.g. Osteoporosis *[1 mark]*

(c) E.g. Regular exercise helps to maintain a healthy weight *[1 mark]*, which reduces the amount of strain placed on joints, helping to prevent damage to them *[1 mark]*.
E.g. Regular exercise can improve the body's ability to repair and strengthen bones *[1 mark]*, which helps to prevent osteoporosis as bones are less likely to become fragile *[1 mark]*.

Page 40: Physical Health — Data Questions

1 (a) 26% *[1 mark]*

(b) E.g. The overall trend is that the proportion of people who smoke in Great Britain is decreasing over time *[1 mark]*.

2 (a) The overall trend is that the percentage of adults that are obese is increasing *[1 mark]*.

(b) E.g. In 2009 the obesity rate for men was lower than the rate for women *[1 mark]*, but in 2010 the rate for men increased sharply and men had a higher obesity rate than women *[1 mark]*. The obesity rate for men decreased between 2010 and 2011, before rising again for two years *[1 mark]*. However, the obesity rate for women consistently declined between 2010 and 2013 *[1 mark]*.

Pages 41-43: Diet, Nutrition and Performance

1 **B** 55-60% carbohydrates, 25-30% fats, 15-20% proteins *[1 mark]*

2 **A** Minerals *[1 mark]*

3

Nutrient	Role in a balanced diet
Fat	Energy for low-intensity exercise
Protein	Repairing muscle
Carbohydrates	**Energy for all intensities of exercise**

[3 marks available in total — 1 mark for each correct entry]

4 (a) Any **two** from: e.g.
• Blood thickening
• Headaches
• Increase in body temperature/heat exhaustion
• Muscle cramps
• Fainting
[2 marks available in total]

(b) E.g. Performers would be at a high risk of dehydration during an endurance event like marathon running *[1 mark]* because this event lasts a very long time, so performers lose a lot of water through sweating and heavy breathing *[1 mark]*.

5 E.g. Protein timing is when a performer consumes protein at certain times to maximise muscle growth — normally one hour after a workout, and just before they go to bed *[1 mark]*. This is necessary because protein is not stored well by the body, so intake must be timed so that protein can be utilised *[1 mark]*. A weightlifter could use protein timing to help gain muscle mass *[1 mark]* which would help them become stronger and lift heavier weights *[1 mark]*.

6 E.g. This is most likely to be the diet of a shot-putter as it has a higher percentage of protein than an average diet *[1 mark]*. Shot-putters require a lot of strength, so need to eat a lot of protein to build muscle mass *[1 mark]*. Both a marathon runner and a long-distance cyclist would require

a larger proportion of carbohydrates and less protein than is shown in Figure 1 *[1 mark]*, because carbohydrates help with endurance, which is more important in these events than muscle mass *[1 mark]*.

7   *This mark scheme gives examples of some points you might have made in your answer, and how many marks you'd get for making those points. You can still get full marks if you haven't written every individual point below, as long as the points you've made are detailed enough.*

You will get up to three marks for showing knowledge and understanding of the roles of fats and carbohydrates in physical activity, for example:

- Fats can be used as energy for low-intensity exercise.
- Carbohydrates can be used as energy for any intensity of exercise.
- Carbohydrate loading is used to increase stores of carbohydrates in the muscles in the days before an event.

You will get up to six marks if you also include examples of how these nutrients affect performance in a marathon, for example:

- A marathon runner would use carbohydrates for energy for the majority of the race, as they are the main energy source for the body.
- A diet too high in fats could cause a marathon runner to gain weight. This would negatively affect their performance in the marathon by reducing their cardiovascular fitness and their speed by increasing the amount of weight they need to carry.
- Fats can be used as an energy source for low-intensity activity, so could be used when running very slowly during a marathon.

You will get up to nine marks if you also evaluate the importance of each nutrient for performance in a marathon, for example:

- Carbohydrates are an essential energy source in a marathon because they can provide energy for all parts of the race, including moderate- and high-intensity parts such as a sprint-finish.
- However, fats still provide a vital function in a balanced diet and help the body to function properly, and can be used as energy in the race if supplies of carbohydrates run out.
- In conclusion, a diet with some fat and plenty of carbohydrates, as well as the use of carbohydrate loading, will help provide essential fuel for performance in a marathon.
[9 marks available in total]

Page 44: Optimum Weight

1   **C** Optimum weight is affected by bone structure, muscle girth, gender and height *[1 mark]*

2   Weight gain occurs when more energy is taken in than is used up by the body — this is known as a **positive** energy balance. To lose weight, more energy must be used up than is taken in — this is known as a **negative** energy balance.
[2 marks available in total — 1 mark for each correct word]

3   (a) Judo *[1 mark]*

(b) E.g. A gymnast will need to be light, as they have to hold their own body weight *[1 mark]*. In judo, being heavy could be an advantage, as it would make a performer harder to throw to the ground *[1 mark]*.

Section Five — Sport Psychology

Page 45: Skills and Practice

1   E.g. Mental rehearsal involves imagining a perfect performance *[1 mark]*, which can help a performer to focus and boost their confidence, so they are able to perform well *[1 mark]*.

2   E.g. A high organisation skill has parts that are closely linked, meaning that it can't easily be broken down into parts that can be practised separately *[1 mark]*.

3   E.g. A closed skill is one that is performed without having to adapt to any external factors *[1 mark]*. The high jump is partially closed, as the jump itself can be practised repeatedly and is usually the same under any conditions *[1 mark]*. However, it is not a completely closed skill, as the run up to the jump can be affected by external factors such as the weather *[1 mark]*.

4   E.g. Distributed practice would be useful for improving a somersault because it is a complex and dangerous skill *[1 mark]*. Distributed practice is well suited for practising this type of skill, as a performer could use the rest breaks for mental rehearsal or to receive feedback *[1 mark]* to avoid injuring themselves when performing a somersault *[1 mark]*.

Page 46: Goal Setting

1   The 'S' in 'SMART' stands for specific, which means a goal should say exactly what the performer wants to achieve *[1 mark]*.

2   (a) E.g. If a goal is measurable, then a performer can see how much they have progressed towards achieving it *[1 mark]*. This can help to motivate a performer to continue training hard *[1 mark]* so that their performance will continue to improve *[1 mark]*.

(b) It specifies a time and a distance, both of which can be accurately measured *[1 mark]*.

(c) E.g. Layla could make her goal time-bound by setting a deadline for when she wants to achieve it, for example, within two months *[1 mark]*. This will help increase her motivation to train, as she will know how much she needs to improve in a certain amount of time *[1 mark]*. Layla could also make sure her goal is achievable by comparing the time in which she can currently run 5 km with the time she wants to achieve *[1 mark]*. This will make sure her goal isn't too difficult for her to achieve, so that she will stay motivated to continue training *[1 mark]*.

Page 47: Guidance and Feedback

1   Mechanical guidance is when a performer is given help with performing a skill through the use of sports equipment *[1 mark]*.

2   Concurrent feedback is given during a performance *[1 mark]*, whereas terminal feedback is given after a performance *[1 mark]*.

3   E.g. Extrinsic feedback comes from a coach or other person *[1 mark]*, which is useful for a beginner as they aren't knowledgeable enough to give themselves feedback *[1 mark]*, so they need someone else to tell them what they are doing right or wrong *[1 mark]*.

88

4 (i) E.g. Verbal guidance can involve a coach giving instructions or descriptions of a skill in words *[1 mark]*, which would be useful for providing instructions to beginners while they are in the pool *[1 mark]*. However, beginners could find this type of guidance confusing if a coach were to use technical language that they were not familiar with *[1 mark]*.

(ii) E.g. Mechanical guidance involves the use of equipment in order to guide a learner through performing a skill, such as armbands or floats in swimming *[1 mark]*. This would be very useful for beginners, who may find it daunting to be in the swimming pool unaided *[1 mark]*, as the use of floats or armbands could help to give them confidence in new swimming skills *[1 mark]*.

Section Six — Sport, Society and Culture

Page 48: Influences on Participation

1 **C** Cost *[1 mark]*

2 E.g. Some sports, like weightlifting, place the body under a lot of strain *[1 mark]*. This means that children should not participate, as their bodies are not developed enough to withstand it *[1 mark]*. Similarly, weightlifting would not be an appropriate sport for the elderly, as the risk of injury will be too high *[1 mark]*.

3 Any **two** from: e.g.
- There may be fewer opportunities through lack of facilities and equipment.
- They may face discrimination or stereotypes about disabled people which may discourage them from taking part.
- The lack of media coverage of disabled sporting events compared to other sporting events may mean there are fewer role models to inspire people to take part.
[2 marks available in total]

4 E.g. Increased media coverage of women's sports could lead to an increase in participation rates amongst women *[1 mark]*, as the media coverage could create role models and also make more women aware of the sports covered *[1 mark]*. This could inspire more women to take part in the sport, and could also challenge stereotypes about women in sport *[1 mark]*.

Page 49: Participation Rates — Data Questions

1 **C** Between 07/08 and 11/12, football was more popular than cycling or running *[1 mark]*

2 (a) Running *[1 mark]*

(b) E.g. Participation in cycling will increase in 13/14 *[1 mark]* because it has increased each year since 10/11, so you would expect the trend to continue *[1 mark]*.

Pages 50-51: Commercialisation of Sport

1 E.g. Sponsorship brings in lots of money that can be spent on developing the sport *[1 mark]*.
E.g. The money brought in through sponsorship may only benefit those at the top of a sport, and not the sport as a whole *[1 mark]*.

2 (a) 2013 *[1 mark]*

(b) £222.9 – £100.45 = £122.45 million *[1 mark]*

3 E.g. Increased media coverage of the Paralympics means that it reaches a wider audience *[1 mark]*. This means that the value of sponsorship deals for the athletes involved may increase *[1 mark]*, as a larger audience means that sponsors can advertise to more people *[1 mark]*.

4 *This mark scheme gives examples of some points you might have made in your answer, and how many marks you'd get for making those points. You can still get full marks if you haven't written every individual point below, as long as the points you've made are detailed enough.*

You will get up to three marks for showing knowledge and understanding of the commercialisation of sport, for example:
- The commercialisation of sport means that there is more money available.
- A lot of this money comes through sponsorship deals, where companies pay to have their logo associated with a team, player or performer.
- Money also comes from the media, who pay for the rights to cover the sport.

You will get up to six marks if you also give effects of commercialisation on players and performers, for example:
- Increased commercialisation of sport has lead to more valuable sponsorship deals for players and performers.
- Commercialisation of sport has lead to increased media attention on players and performers.
- Commercialisation of sport means the media can control when and how often sporting events take place.

You will get up to nine marks if you also evaluate whether the impact of commercialisation on players and performers has been positive or negative, for example:
- Commercialisation has had some positive impact on players and performers, for example, very high earnings due to the increase in the value of sponsorship deals. However, sponsorship deals mean that they may have to appear in adverts and endorse products, even if they don't want to.
- Other negative effects of commercialisation include the lack of privacy players and performers experience due to media coverage of their private lives. The media's control of how often matches are played can also impact players and performers negatively, as it means they could be more likely to get injured.
- In conclusion, commercialisation has had a positive impact on players and performers. Although they have to sacrifice some of their privacy, they can now earn large amounts of money and can therefore play their sport full-time.
[9 marks available in total]

Page 52: Sporting Behaviour

1 **D** Deliberately tripping a player as they run down the pitch in hockey *[1 mark]*

2 (a) E.g. Sportsmanship means being honest, sticking to the rules and treating your opponents with respect *[1 mark]*.

(b) E.g. In football, players will kick the ball out of play if an opposition player is injured *[1 mark]*.

3 E.g. If professional athletes are caught cheating they face very strict punishments and may also receive negative coverage in the media *[1 mark]*. However, professional athletes may still be tempted to commit deviance, because winning is worth so much to them in terms of prize money, sponsorship and potential fame *[1 mark]*. Amateur athletes

may be less likely to commit deviance because they have far less to gain *[1 mark]*. However, amateur athletes are less likely to be caught and punished than professionals, so may be more willing than professionals to risk committing deviance *[1 mark]*.

Page 53: Sporting Behaviour — Data Questions

1 (a)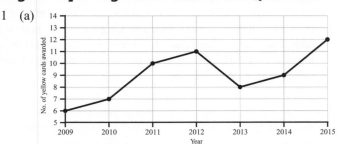

[2 marks available in total — 1 mark for correctly plotting the points and joining them with straight lines and 1 mark for labelling the axes]

(b) E.g. The fine was initially successful but its effectiveness seems to have worn off *[1 mark]* because there was a decrease in the number of yellow cards awarded in 2013, but in 2015 the number of yellow cards awarded was higher than in 2012 *[1 mark]*.

(c) E.g. The number of yellow cards in 2016 will increase *[1 mark]* because the number has increased in each of the previous two years *[1 mark]*.

Practice Papers

Pages 54-68: Component 1 Practice Paper

1 (a) **C** Tibia *[1 mark]*

(b) **B** Hamstrings *[1 mark]*

(c) **D** The effort is between the fulcrum and load *[1 mark]*

(d) **A** Flexion *[1 mark]*

(e) **C** Cardiovascular fitness *[1 mark]*

(f) **D** Circuit training *[1 mark]*

(g) **A** Erythropoietin (EPO) *[1 mark]*

(h) **C** Above Average *[1 mark]*

2 E.g. Tendons attach muscle to bone *[1 mark]*. When muscles contract, the tendons pull the bones to move the skeleton *[1 mark]*.

3 E.g. The antagonistic muscle pair at the knee works to push the athlete's body weight off the floor *[1 mark]* as the quadriceps contract *[1 mark]* and the hamstrings relax *[1 mark]*.

To explain what the muscle pair does to help the athlete to jump, you could have said that it moves the knee from flexion to extension instead.
The antagonistic muscle pair at the knee isn't the only one you could have written about — there's also the pair at the hip (the gluteus maximus and hip flexors), or at the ankle (the gastrocnemius and tibialis anterior).

4 (a) Type IIX *[1 mark]*

(b) E.g. During the long jump, the athlete would need to sprint quickly and jump powerfully *[1 mark]*, so type IIX fibres would be most suitable because they can contract with the greatest force *[1 mark]*.

5 A lever with a mechanical advantage can move a large load with a small effort *[1 mark]*. However, it only allows a small range of movement *[1 mark]*.

6 E.g. Vascular shunting occurs when the arteries supplying the working muscles vasodilate *[1 mark]* and arteries supplying inactive areas of the body vasoconstrict *[1 mark]*. This causes the amount of blood flowing to the muscles used during exercise to increase *[1 mark]*.

7 (i) E.g Anaerobic respiration can release energy very quickly for short periods *[1 mark]*, allowing a performer to sprint through the water *[1 mark]*. This makes it very useful during races of a short distance, or in parts of longer races, such as a sprint finish *[1 mark]*.

(ii) E.g. Anaerobic respiration releases lactic acid as a by-product *[1 mark]*, which would eventually lead to muscle fatigue *[1 mark]*, so it can't be sustained for a long period *[1 mark]*.

8 E.g. An increase in breathing rate would increase the rate that oxygen is delivered into the lungs *[1 mark]*. An increase in heart rate would increase the rate that blood passes through the capillaries in the lungs and is delivered to the muscles *[1 mark]*. Therefore, when both breathing rate and heart rate increase, oxygen can diffuse much more quickly from the lungs into the bloodstream *[1 mark]* and then be delivered to the muscles to be used to release energy *[1 mark]*.

9 (a) Second class *[1 mark]*

(b) E.g. The load is the diver's body weight, which is in the middle of the lever arm, therefore it is a second class lever *[1 mark]*.

10 (i) E.g. He may have been jogging lightly to warm up *[1 mark]* because his heart rate increases for 10 minutes, then stays at a moderate rate *[1 mark]*.

(ii) E.g. He may have increased his running speed and then continued to run at this speed *[1 mark]*, because his heart rate increases very quickly and stays elevated to this level between 20 and 50 minutes *[1 mark]*.

11 E.g. Regular exercise makes the heart stronger and increases the size of its ventricles, therefore increasing maximum stroke volume and cardiac output *[1 mark]*. This would increase the amount of oxygenated blood reaching the muscles of an endurance athlete *[1 mark]*, meaning they would be able to exercise more intensely and for longer *[1 mark]*.

12 E.g. The third class lever used by the tennis player allows her to move the tennis racquet quickly *[1 mark]* and through a large range of movement *[1 mark]* in order to generate lots of power with the swing *[1 mark]*.

13 E.g. Flexibility is the amount of movement possible at a joint *[1 mark]*. Having a high level of flexibility in, for example, the hip joint, would help a long jumper to reach their legs further *[1 mark]*, and therefore jump a greater distance *[1 mark]*.

14 (i) E.g. The sit and reach test measures flexibility of the back and lower hamstrings *[1 mark]*, which could be useful for a beach volleyball player if they need to reach high to serve or dive for the ball *[1 mark]*. However, it is not the most important fitness test for a beach volleyball player, as flexibility of the shoulders is much more important for most actions in beach volleyball *[1 mark]*.

Answers

(ii) E.g. The vertical jump test measures power of the leg muscles *[1 mark]*, therefore it is a useful fitness test for a beach volleyball player *[1 mark]* as they would need power in their legs to jump high when spiking the ball *[1 mark]*.

15 (a) E.g. A course must be set out using cones, and the person taking the test must start the course by lying down at the first cone. They must then run as quickly as possible around the course, weaving around the cones first in one direction, then the other, before running to the final cone.
[2 marks for a complete description,
1 mark for a partial description]

(b) E.g. The time taken to complete the Illinois agility run test is decreasing, which means her agility is increasing *[1 mark]*. Her time on the 30 m sprint test is decreasing, which means she is running faster *[1 mark]*.

(c) Any **one** from:
• Yoga
• Pilates
[1 mark available]

16 (a) Progressive overload means gradually increasing the amount of overload done in training to increase fitness without risk of injury *[1 mark]*.

(b) E.g. If a javelin thrower used weight training, they could gradually increase the weight lifted *[1 mark]* in order to increase their strength *[1 mark]*.

17 (a) $220 - 40 = 180$ bpm *[1 mark]*

(b) Upper anaerobic threshold:
180×0.9 *[1 mark]* $= 162$ bpm *[1 mark]*
Lower anaerobic threshold:
180×0.8 *[1 mark]* $= 144$ bpm *[1 mark]*

18 E.g. Rugby players can avoid injury by following the rules of the sport, for example, by tackling safely *[1 mark]*. The rules are in place to ensure safety and protect players from injury *[1 mark]*.
E.g. Rugby players can avoid injury by wearing the recommended protective equipment, such as shin pads or a scrum cap *[1 mark]*. Protective equipment is designed to protect the most vulnerable areas in that sport *[1 mark]*.

19 Anabolic steroids would give the most significant performance benefit to a 100 m sprinter *[1 mark]* as they increase muscle growth and therefore strength *[1 mark]*, which sprinters need in order to generate the necessary power to sprint quickly *[1 mark]*.

20 *This mark scheme gives examples of some points you might have made in your answer, and how many marks you would get for making those points. You can still get full marks if you haven't written every individual point below, as long as the points you have made are detailed enough.*

You will get up to three marks for showing knowledge and understanding of tidal volume, for example:

• Tidal volume is the volume of air breathed in or out during one breath.
• Increased tidal volume brings more oxygen into the lungs.
• Increased tidal volume removes more carbon dioxide from the lungs.

You will get up to six marks if you also include examples from a football match that would impact on the need for a midfielder to have an increased tidal volume, for example:

• A slight increase in tidal volume would help a midfielder to meet the increased oxygen demand in the muscles, and so release the energy needed to jog around the pitch throughout the match.
• A large increase in tidal volume would help a midfielder to remove lactic acid from the muscles and recover from oxygen debt after sprinting up the pitch.
• An increase in tidal volume would be less beneficial to a midfielder during actions such as taking a penalty, as this action would not require much extra energy to be released in the muscles and therefore would not lead to much of an increase in oxygen demand.

You will get up to nine marks if you also make judgements about the extent to which an increase in tidal volume will allow a midfielder to perform well in a football match, for example:

• An increase in tidal volume would be necessary to bring in extra oxygen and remove extra carbon dioxide, as running around the pitch for 90 minutes would increase the rate of respiration in the muscles.
• Other changes would also be necessary to meet the increased oxygen demand in the muscles, for example, increased heart rate, stroke volume and breathing rate.
• In conclusion, without an increase in tidal volume, a midfielder would be unable to remain active for the total duration of a match. However, this change alone would be insufficient to meet the demands of the match, therefore other physiological changes would also be necessary.
[9 marks available in total]

21 *This mark scheme gives examples of some points you might have made in your answer, and how many marks you would get for making those points. You can still get full marks if you haven't written every individual point below, as long as the points you have made are detailed enough.*

You will get up to three marks for showing knowledge and understanding of fartlek training and plyometric training, for example:

• Fartlek training involves varying the intensity of exercise.
• The intervals in fartlek training don't have a strict structure.
• Plyometric training involves actions such as jumping.

You will get up to six marks if you also include examples of how these training methods can be used to improve performance in netball, for example:

• Fartlek training can be used to develop muscular endurance and cardiovascular fitness, which a netball player would need to perform well for the duration of a game.
• Fartlek training can improve speed, which a netball player would need to quickly get into position when receiving a pass.
• Plyometric training would help improve power in the leg muscles, which a netball player would need to jump powerfully to intercept a pass, or to sprint down the court.

You will get up to nine marks if you also make judgements about the suitability of these training methods for a netball player, for example:

• Fartlek training would be a very useful training method for improving netball performance, as it could be adapted to replicate the changing pace of a netball match.
• Although plyometric training would be useful for improving a netball player's ability to jump and sprint

powerfully, it would not improve their cardiovascular fitness and ability to be perform well throughout the duration of a match.

- In conclusion, both fartlek training and plyometric training would be useful for improving performance in netball. However, plyometric training alone would be insufficient to improve overall performance, so a player may want to use a combination of both methods.
[9 marks available in total]

Pages 69-79: Component 2 Practice Paper

1 (a) **B** Increasing carbohydrate intake before an endurance event *[1 mark]*

(b) **C** Achievable *[1 mark]*

(c) **C** Feedback that is received after a performance *[1 mark]*

(d) **D** Socio-economic *[1 mark]*

(e) **A** Time-wasting in football *[1 mark]*

(f) **B** 25 to 44 *[1 mark]*

2 (a) E.g. Improved efficiency of the cardiovascular system *[1 mark]*.
There are lots of other benefits that you could put here, like improved body tone, increased strength, increased flexibility and better posture.

(b) E.g. Exercise increases the level of endorphins in your brain *[1 mark]*. This helps you to feel good, so can help prevent depression *[1 mark]*.
You could also have explained how exercise helps to reduce stress, or how it helps improve confidence and gives a sense of achievement.

(c) Social *[1 mark]*

3 E.g. Smoking damages the alveoli, so they work less effectively *[1 mark]*. This means that a swimmer would not be able to get as much oxygen to their muscles as quickly, so would not be able to work as intensely and may have difficulty breathing during swimming *[1 mark]*.

E.g. Smoking damages cilia in the windpipe, so increases the chance of infection *[1 mark]*. This means that a swimmer is more likely to get ill, which would mean they would miss training, which could cause a drop in performance *[1 mark]*.

4 (a) E.g. Dehydration can cause the blood to become **thicker**. It can also cause your body temperature to **increase**.
[2 marks available in total — 1 mark for each correct word]
You will still get the marks for using other words that mean the same thing — e.g. if you say 'more viscous' instead of 'thicker'.

(b) Any **one** from: e.g.
- Exercise causes heavier breathing.
- Exercise causes increased sweating.
[1 mark available]

5 (a) Rugby *[1 mark]*

(b) E.g. The rugby players' optimum weights are also affected by their height, bone structure, muscle girth and the position they play *[1 mark]*. So, for example, the players could have different optimum weights because they are a different height *[1 mark]*.

(c) E.g. The energy balance is the relationship between the amount of energy you get from food and the amount of energy you use up *[1 mark]*. To increase weight, the hockey player's energy intake (from food) would need to be greater than the amount of energy they use up, giving them a positive energy balance *[1 mark]*.

6 (i) E.g. Variable practice is important in tennis because tennis involves mainly open skills *[1 mark]*. Variable practice will provide practice in many different match situations — for example, allowing a player to react to different types of shot *[1 mark]* — which will provide realistic practice and therefore help improve their performance in a real match *[1 mark]*.

(ii) E.g. Fixed practice is less important in tennis as there are fewer closed skills in the sport, although it still plays an important role in coaching a player's serve *[1 mark]*. Fixed practice would only provide repeated practice of skills in the same situations *[1 mark]*, so would not provide realistic practice for many of the skills needed in a match *[1 mark]*.

7 E.g. Amanda's goal applies the time-bound principle by saying that she wants to achieve her goal in four months *[1 mark]*. Having a deadline will help motivate her to train *[1 mark]* and will therefore improve her fitness and performance so she will be more likely to achieve her goal *[1 mark]*.

8 (a) The trend is that participation in swimming is decreasing *[1 mark]*.

(b) E.g. More women participate in swimming than men *[1 mark]*. This could be because there are more female role models in swimming than male role models *[1 mark]*. E.g. More men participate in football than women *[1 mark]*. This could be because women have faced discrimination for wanting to play football *[1 mark]*.

9 (a) E.g. For some people from certain ethnic groups there may be a lack of role models in sport *[1 mark]*. This could lead some people to be less inspired to participate in sport themselves *[1 mark]*.

(b) Any **one** from: e.g.
- Age
- Socio-economic group
- Disability
[1 mark available]

10 (a) E.g. An alcoholic drinks company *[1 mark]*.

(b) E.g. As it is a youth tournament, the participants are young so may be impressionable *[1 mark]*. This means that the company's sponsorship might make them more likely to start underage drinking, which would have a negative impact on their health *[1 mark]*.

11 (i) E.g. Increased media coverage can have a positive impact on a sport by increasing awareness of the sport and helping it to reach a wider audience *[1 mark]*. This could lead to an increase in participation in the sport *[1 mark]* and increased ticket revenues from more people coming to watch events *[1 mark]*.

(ii) E.g. Increased media coverage of a sport could have a negative impact as the media may come to have too much control over the sport *[1 mark]*. As the sport becomes increasingly reliant on the money brought in through media coverage, this puts the media companies in a position of power *[1 mark]* which could lead to the media dictating when and how many games are played, and maybe even changing the rules of the sport *[1 mark]*.

12 (a) E.g. Gamesmanship is gaining an advantage by using tactics that seem unfair, but aren't against the rules *[1 mark]*.

  (b) E.g. Elite performers demonstrating gamesmanship could be bad for the sport as it could lead to more occurrences of gamesmanship at lower levels of the sport *[1 mark]*. This is because elite performers are role models and cricket is a high-profile sport *[1 mark]*, so their behaviour will gain lots of media attention and may inspire others to behave in the same way *[1 mark]*.

13 *This mark scheme gives examples of some points you might have made in your answer, and how many marks you would get for making those points. You can still get full marks if you haven't written every individual point below, as long as the points you have made are detailed enough.*

You will get up to three marks for showing knowledge and understanding of carbohydrate loading and timing of protein intake, for example:

- Carbohydrates provide energy for all intensities of exercise.
- Carbohydrate loading is when a performer increases their intake of carbohydrates a few days before an event to increase the amount of energy stored in their muscles.
- Timing of protein intake means eating protein at certain times, e.g. within an hour of working out or just before bed, to maximise muscle growth.

You will get up to six marks if you also include examples of how these dietary techniques can affect the performance of a long-distance cyclist, for example:

- Carbohydrate loading can help a long-distance cyclist because it is a long duration event, so they will need a lot of energy.
- A long-distance cyclist needs large leg muscles to generate enough power, e.g. for steep hills and to sprint at the finish. Correct timing of protein intake can promote muscle hypertrophy of the leg muscles.
- A long-distance cyclist may want to limit their use of protein timing, because increasing their muscle mass would make them heavier which would mean they use up more energy.

You will get up to nine marks if you also evaluate whether a combination of these two techniques can improve a long-distance cyclist's performance, for example:

- Carbohydrate loading is vital for a long-distance cyclist, as they need to have enough energy stored in their muscles to last the length of the race.
- Timing of protein intake could be useful as part of a cyclist's training, as it will help them to develop powerful leg muscles. However, too much muscle mass could make them too heavy to ride efficiently.
- In conclusion, a long-distance cyclist should use a combination of carbohydrate loading and timing of protein intake to improve their race performance, as long as they do not gain too much muscle mass and become too heavy and exceed their optimum weight for the event.

[9 marks available in total]

14 *This mark scheme gives examples of some points you might have made in your answer, and how many marks you would get for making those points. You can still get full marks if you haven't written every individual point below, as long as the points you have made are detailed enough.*

You will get up to three marks for showing knowledge and understanding of visual and mechanical guidance, for example:

- Visual guidance involves being shown visually how to perform a skill.
- Visual guidance can include demonstrations or videos of skills being performed.
- Mechanical guidance involves the use of equipment to help a learner perform a skill.

You will get up to six marks if you also apply your knowledge of these guidance types to a group of beginners in trampolining, for example:

- Visual guidance could be used to demonstrate how basic bounces on the trampoline should look.
- Mechanical guidance could include the use of a harness to guide the learners through a somersault on the trampoline.
- A coach could use both guidance types in a session, for example, allowing learners to watch a somersault being performed before attempting it themselves using mechanical guidance.

You will get up to nine marks if you also evaluate the use of the guidance types for beginners in trampolining, for example:

- Mechanical guidance can be very useful for a learner in trampolining, as it can increase their confidence at performing dangerous or complex skills. However, it should be removed as soon as it is safe to, so that the beginners do not depend on it.
- Visual guidance would be useful for the beginners who aren't familiar with different trampolining skills. However, it may not help them to fully learn the skill as some trampolining skills may be too complex to copy from a demonstration.
- In conclusion, it may be best for visual guidance to be used initially so that the beginners become familiar with what trampolining skills should look like, before using mechanical guidance to help them learn the skill.

[9 marks available in total]

Answers